LIVING

AKIVA
TATZ

INSPIRED

TARGUM/FELDHEIM

First published 1993

Copyright © 1993 by A. Tatz
ISBN 1-56871-026-7

Phototypeset at Targum Press

Printing plates by Frank, Jerusalem

Published by:
Targum Press Inc.
22700 W. Eleven Mile Rd.
Southfield, Mich. 48034

in conjunction with
Mishnas Rishonim

Distributed by:
Feldheim Publishers
200 Airport Executive Park
Spring Valley, N.Y. 10977

Distributed in Israel by:
Targum Press Ltd.
POB 43170
Jerusalem 91430

Printed in Israel

For Joseph and Hannah Katz שיח׳

בית מדרש למורות

BETH MIDRASH LEMOROTH

Founded by Mr A. KOHN

Principal: Rabbi M. MILLER

50, BEWICK ROAD
GATESHEAD NE8 4DQ
Telephone: 091-477 2620
091-477 1566

ב״ה

Av 5753.

Dr. Akiva Tatz has accorded me the privilege of studying the manuscript of his latest work, *Living Inspired,* a work which is indeed an impressive accomplishment.

It is a work of profundity and inspiration and one wonders whether the modern frenetic westernized world is attuned to such depth of thought.

Confusion of philosophic opinions and beliefs will only be resolved by reaching the single source of all diversity, a source elusive to so many.

Dr. Tatz has already enlightened and inspired so many worldwide by his spoken and written word and now again provides us with spiritual enrichment, employing his power of incisive and penetrating thought to search out the depths of Torah tradition — the source of all that is "life and good." His presentation is imbued with clarity and sensitivity so that the intelligent reader will find it enlightening to the mind and warming to the heart.

I highly recommend this masterpiece to all who seek to discover the essence of Judaism and, in effect, their true selves.

Rabbi M. Miller

בס"ד

כתיב "וכתבת על האבנים את כל דברי התורה הזאת באר היטב" ותנן בריש פ' אלו
נאמרין (סוטה ל"ב.) הביאו את האבנים ובנו את המזבח וסדוהו בסיד וכתבו עליו
את כל דברי התורה בשבעים לשון שנא' באר היטב, והנה רבים ממוני המצוות
(הבה"ג רס"ג וסיעתם) מנו מצוה זו בכלל תרי"ג, והרמב"ם בשורש השלישי דחה
דבריהם וע"ש ברמב"ן וז"ל אבל המצוות שענינים קיים לנו לדורות ימנה אותם אע"פ
שאינם נעשות אלא פעם אחת, ולכן מנה פרשת אבנים גדולות לפי שנצטוינו לכתוב
בהם התורה באר היטב בשבעים לשון להיותם לנו זכר לדורות עכ"ל, ועיי' בסה"מ
לרס"ג סוף פ' ס'. וכפי הנראה ענין המצוה שתהי' התורה כתובה בשבעים לשון עבור
רחוקים בכל מרחק שהוא שיוכלו ללמדה ותמצא להם מסילה לתורה דרך כל לשון
והבנה שהיא, וחובתינו כמקבלי התורה להעמידה בעולם כך, שתהי' בת גישה לכל
הרוצה ללמדה באמת, ועיין בסוטה ל"ה:

והנה מאז שנפרצו כל חומותינו ותרגומי התורה החשיכו עינינו, נתרחקנו מקיום
מצוה זו, ואין בידינו להעתיק אמיתת צורת דברי תורה ללשונות אחרים, ואין
עומקה ויפי' של תורה מתגלים אלא בד' אמות של ביהמ"ד פנימה, לעוסקים בה
כנתינתה, והיו הדברים האלה בהוייתן יהיו.

אבל מה נעשה והדברים מוכחים שחייבים אנו להשתדל במלאכת תרגום דברי
תורה ואף זה בכלל עת לעשות לה' הפרו תורתיך, כי רבים הם שהמאור הזה הקורן
ומאיר מרחוק מאורו של תורה מחזירם למוטב ולדרכה של תורה. והנה ידידי
הנעלה הרב מו"ה עקיבא ד"ר טץ שליט"א שיודע אני בו כי מבני בית המדרש הוא
והבנתנו ישרה ותפיסתו בד"ת עדינה ונכונה, וכבר איתמחי גברא ועושה הוא גדולות
ונצורות בהשבת רבים לתורה ע"י העתקת דברי תורה והלבשתם בלשון דהאידנא,
כפי צורת הדברים המתבארת בספר זה, ונפלאה היא השפעת דברים אלו על
שומעיהם, והנה ספר זה נכתב בעקרו עבור אותם הזקוקים לתרגום ולהעתקה,
ועבורם השכיל המשכיל ידידי הנ"ל הרהמ"ח שליט"א ברב כשרון ובטוב טעם ודעת להעתיק
גם משהו מרומה ועומקה של תורה, ואשרי חלקו. ויהי רצון מלפני נותן התורה ית'
שיועיל ספר זה לבאים בשעריו כפי שהועילו הדברים כאשר נאמרו ע"פ, להאיר
באורה של תורה ויתקים מה' משהו מאותה מצוה שנצטוינו קודם ביאת הארץ
וכתבת וגו' את כל דברי התורה הזאת באר היטב בשבעים לשון, ובמהרה תחזינה
עינינו כי יכירו וידעו כל יושבי תבל כי לך תכרע כל ברך תשבע כל לשון.

והנני חותם לכבוד ידידי הרהמ"ח ששם שמים מתקדש ומתאהב על ידו.

בברכה

משה שפירא

משה שפירא

Letter of Approbation from Rabbi Moshe Shapira שליט"א

לע״נ

דבורה פעסא בת צבי אריה ז״ל   רייזל בת לייב ז״ל
Mrs. Devorah Kirsh   Mrs. Rose Bacher

Dedicated by their children
Issie and Mushe Kirsh

and their grandchildren
Jonathan and Louise Bortz,
William Kirsh, Daniel Kirsh,
Kevin and Jacqueline Lampert

Dedicated by the

South African Jewish Community
to
Ohr Somayach of South Africa

*in recognition of their educational
and inspirational contribution to
the community.*

בס״ד

לע״נ אבי מורי
קאפל בן עקיבא אריה ז״ל
ת.נ.צ.ב.ה.

Acknowledgments

Virtually nothing in this book is original. Sources other than those quoted directly in the text are Rabbi Moshe Shapira, Rabbi Mordechai Miller and Rabbi Yitzchok Zev Josef, שליט״א.

The following people provided invaluable assistance and I thank them:

* My mother, Mrs. Minde Tatz for expert work on the manuscript;
* My brother-in-law and sister, Ian and Anna-Louise Shapiro for general support;
* Philip Feitelberg for the photograph of a Jerusalem stairway which graces the cover;
* Dr. Jack Cohen for masterful technical assistance;
* Jonathan Mayer for accurate research;
* The staff of Targum Press for exceptional courtesy and efficiency;
* My wife, Suzanne, who makes living inspired easy for all who know her;
* Rabbi Larry Shain, Rabbi Shmuel Moffson and Rabbi Yechezkel Auerbach of Ohr Somayach South Africa who built the forum in which much of the material in this book was developed and refined.

A.T.
Av 5753
August 1993

Contents

Introduction

The purpose of this book is to provide, in some small way, a guide to inspiration. Our generation is characterized by anxiety and terror; and often the root of these emotions is existential — a lack of sense of purpose and direction. Most modern Jews lack a basic knowledge of Torah structure, Torah definition of the pattern of the world. With no organized frame of reference the world seems haphazard and arbitrary, and one cannot generate any semblance of inner peace, let alone serenity, if one's inner life is built on emotional and mental quicksand.

While it is true that there are many things we cannot understand, there is plenty that we can. A Torah framework provides the structure and stability for approaching life in general and particularly life's problems and traumas in a meaningful and organized way. Instead of fearing each day's unpredictability and living in a constant vacuum of apprehension, we should aim to be surging ahead in personal growth, secure in the knowledge that everything has an underlying structure and meaning and that ultimately every detail of life is eminently worthwhile and of cosmic significance. Such an approach to life generates happiness.

The first chapter of this book contains a description of one basic theme at the root of the deeper wisdom of Torah. The words are necessarily clumsy, in fact there are no words for pure abstraction; what is needed is a sensitivity on the part of the reader to penetrate beyond the words into the meaning which can never be expressed in finite words. (This idea itself is examined in more detail later.) A remarkable feature of the deeper wisdom is that when it is absorbed, one finds that in fact one knew it already. *"Ha'emes eid l'atzmo* — The truth is a witness to itself" — where "truth" is a codeword for the inner truth; it does not have to be learned, only *recognized*. All deeper wisdom is none other than a *description* of some or other aspect of reality.

The purpose of this book is *not* to explore the mystical world in technical detail but rather to explore *where the deeper pattern expresses itself* in explicit reality and *particularly in our life experiences and ordeals*. Therefore the first chapter defines only the most basic roots of a pattern which we will be able to apply consistently.

The subsequent chapters each analyze a critically important area of our lives, both our individual inner lives and our interactions in relationships, using the same basic structure and principles. Correctly understanding that all of life is based on the same fundamental unity of pattern is itself enough to generate *emuna*, faith, in the overriding Unity of reality. With a core of deep *emuna*, existential anxiety and a sense of agonized, meaningless drifting from the fear of one ordeal to the next are impossible. The pathway to serenity has begun, and with the personality tools of *emuna*, happiness and an inspired sense of purpose, one can begin life's work of achieving spiritual greatness.

A warning: each chapter introduces a central issue or concept. *Each of these* is needed to fully appreciate *any of the others*, since each is fundamental to spiritual living. Therefore in order to successfully integrate the material presented here each chapter must be studied with all the others in mind and being brought to bear upon it constantly — reading the whole book in sequence twice is the best way to do this.

I.

Pattern
of
Life

Chapter 1

Higher Pattern

A ccording to our received tradition, the world is built on a pattern which permeates its *every detail*. This pattern has many ramifications, enfoldings on itself and details within details which in fact are endless; however for purposes of our discussion let us trace only one aspect of one basic facet of this pattern.

Put most fundamentally, this pattern has three elements. In the life-issues which we shall examine together in subsequent chapters we shall sometimes be focusing on the interaction between the first two, sometimes the second two and sometimes all three, but *all of them* will be found *everywhere*. One cannot always speak out every detail and you will be left with the challenge of amplifying each subject to fully express the pattern in each; this exercise itself is a Torah-learning experience and immensely rewarding.

A description of these basic elements is necessarily difficult and vague — there are no words for pure essence. Mystical truths can only be talked "around", *until one "falls in"*! When one suddenly grasps the essence it is seen to be incandescent with clarity and remarkably simple, but it must be grasped inwardly, it can never be entirely expressed.

Put most simply, the three elements are as follows.

The first is the point of beginning, the transition from nothing to something. It is variously expressed as the moment of creation, the male experience or pole of reality, the number one, the right hand; and is embodied in the person of Avraham Avinu (Abraham). It is the pristine flash of energy which begins any process. It is by definition indivisible. The Torah expresses this by referring to the first day of Creation thus: "And it was evening and it was morning, *yom echad* — day one." It does *not* state "the *first* day" as a parallel to the subsequent "the *second* day", "the *third* day", because in its pure being at the root of Creation it is not *first*, part of an unfolding process of differentiation, it is simply "one".

The second is the process itself, the condensing of creative energy into tangible form. It is the expansion of the flash of beginning into finite form. It is expressed as the female dimension, the number two, the left hand; and is embodied in Yitzchak Avinu (Isaac).

These two energies are paradoxical and antithetical. The first is related to infinity, the second finite. The first is indivisible oneness, the second all fragmentation. No two concepts could possibly be more opposite, more mutually exclusive. And that leads to the mystery of the third: it is the resolution of this cosmic tension. The third element is the harmony of opposites; but its mystery and magic are that at a deeper level it reveals that in fact there never was a conflict. Both the first and second dimensions are melted into a new reality, a reality which somehow unifies them and yet allows each to be fully expressed in its own right. Of the three, this is perhaps the most difficult to express in words; it can only be experienced. It is however alluded to as harmony, balance, the return to source, truth, true marriage, the number three, the center of the body; and is the energy of Yaakov Avinu (Jacob) in the world.

As explained previously, the purpose of this discussion is not to trace the roots and branches of these ideas but to understand their application in the world of human experience. In terms of emotions, the first element is essentially pleasurable; it contains the thrill of new creation, the revelation of something previously hidden. The second necessarily involves work and pain; it contains the pain of infinite potential shrinking to finite proportions, the sacrifice of all the creative energy which could not be crystallized into limited space and time, the pain of separation from a pure origin. The third is true, mature human joy. It is the happiness of the resolution of doubts, the depth of emotion felt upon understanding why what seemed cruelty was in fact kindness. It is the joy of well-earned reward. The natural mode of the first phase is ecstasy, of the second pain, and of the third, transcendence.

An examination of one application of this system will help to make it tangible. In describing these things the mystical sources talk about the body. Of course they are referring to a higher reality, but since the physical is an exactly accurate projection of the spiritual, we can work with the physical and understand the spiritual. If we consider male and female physically, biologically, we see illustrated all that we have alluded to thus far. The development of a human being, perhaps the ultimate process in the world, requires father and mother. The male contribution is infinitesimally small in space and time, it consists of the contribution of a genetic code and no more. It involves no work and no pain. It is simply the flash of beginning. The female dimension, however, is opposite. It involves an expansion in space and time — the child is formed physically within the mother, over considerable time. Effort and pain are involved. The tiny gift of a code of genes is crystallized into tangible form within her body. And finally, a child is born — both father and mother have melted into one in this child, each unique component now blended into a third, a new human being who transcends from one generation to another.

This model of man and woman and their interaction, at all levels — biologically, emotionally and spiritually — should be kept in mind as the central illustration of the pattern we are studying. This pattern is the root; all else is application.

Chapter 2

Inspiration and Disappointment
(or Why a Good Time Never Lasts)

The natural pathway of all life experiences begins with inspiration and soon fades to disappointment. Let us analyze this phenomenon and understand it.

Human consciousness and human senses are tuned to an initial burst of sensitivity and then rapidly decay into dullness. Sights, sounds, smells, even tactile stimuli are felt sharply at first and then hardly at all — a constant sound is not registered; one suddenly becomes aware that it was present when it stops! We are incapable of maintaining the freshness of any experience naturally — only in the dimension of miracle is that possible: the sacrificial bread in the *Beis Hamikdash,* the Temple, remained steaming fresh permanently to manifest the constant freshness of Hashem's relationship with the Jewish people. The natural pathway is that things which are fresh become stale.

One of the Torah sources for this idea lies in the sequence

of events surrounding the exodus from Egypt. At an extremely low point in our history, during the intense misery of slavery in Egypt, literally at the point of spiritual annihilation, the Jewish people were uplifted miraculously. Ten plagues revealed Hashem's presence and might, culminating in a night of unprecedented revelation with the tenth. This spiritual high was amplified by many orders of magnitude at the splitting of the sea — there the lowliest of the Jewish people experienced more than the highest prophet subsequently. And suddenly, once through the sea, they were deposited in a desert with forty-nine days of work ahead of them to climb to the spiritual status of meriting the Sinai experience, the giving of the Torah. Mystically, a desert means a place of intense death-forces, a place of lethal ordeals. No water means no life. (And we see later the potency of the ordeals which faced them in the desert.) *

What is the meaning of this pattern? The idea is that in order to save the Jewish people in Egypt outside help was necessary. Hashem appeared and elevated us spiritually *although we did not deserve it intrinsically, we had not yet earned it*. But once saved,

---

* There are mystical sources which state that the plagues in Egypt were ten in number in order to destroy the ten dimensions of evil with which the Egyptians had "contaminated" the ten sayings of Creation (and hence occurred in reverse order: the Creation developed from an infinite point in concentric layers, as it were, and the plagues reversed this order to peel away the layers of impurity from the outside to arrive eventually at a pure center — the first saying of Creation was "In the beginning"; the last plague was destruction of the firstborn, the manifestation of "firstness", of new creation; the second saying was "Let there be light"; the second-last plague was darkness! And these sources proceed to work out the entire sequence thus). However, in the desert the Jewish people faced ten trials, each representing a battle with one of the ten dimensions of evil on a cosmic scale, their challenge being to defeat all evil on their journey to holiness and thereby return the world to its perfection; had they succeeded they would have arrived at the borders of Israel able to usher in the final and permanent redemption with their entry into the Land. The desert, in other words, is the dimension of cosmically concentrated evil.

once inspired, once made conscious of our higher reality, the price must be paid, the experience must be earned, and in working to earn the level which was previously given *artificially*, one *acquires* that level genuinely. Instead of being *shown* a spiritual level, one *becomes* it.

And that is the secret of life. A person is inspired artificially at the beginning of any phase of life, but to acquire the depth of personality which is demanded of us, Hashem *removes the inspiration*. The danger is apathy and depression; the challenge is to fight back to the point of inspiration, and in so doing to *build it permanently into one's character*. The plagues in Egypt and the splitting of the sea are dazzling beyond description, but then Hashem puts us in the desert and challenges us to fight through to Sinai. In Egypt He demonstrates destruction of ten levels of evil while we watch passively; in the desert He brings ten levels of evil to bear against us and challenges *us* to destroy them.

This idea recurs everywhere. Pesach occurs in Nissan — the zodiac of this month is the sheep, an animal which is passively led. Next comes Iyar — the ox, an animal which has its own wilful strength. And thereafter comes Sivan — twins, perfect harmony. It is like a father teaching his child to walk: first the father supports the child as he takes his first step, but then the father must let go; there is no other way to learn, and the child must take a frightened and lonely step unaided. Only then, when he can walk independently, can he feel his father's love in the very moment which previously felt like desertion.

Unfortunately most people do not know this secret. We are misled into thinking that the world is supposed to be a constant thrill and we feel only half-alive because it is not. Let us examine some applications of this fundamental principle.

In *aggadic* writings we are told that the unborn child is taught the whole Torah in the womb. An angel teaches him all the mysteries of Creation and all that he will ever need to know in order to reach perfection, his own *chelek* (portion) in Torah. A lamp is lit above his head, and by its light he sees from one end of the world to the other. As the child is born, however, the angel strikes him on the mouth and he forgets all that he has learned and is born a simple and unlearned baby. The obvious question is: why teach a child so much and then cause all the teaching to be forgotten?

But the answer is that it is not forgotten; it is driven deep into the unconscious. A person may be born with no explicit knowledge, but beneath the conscious surface, intact and rich beyond imagination, is *all that one wishes to know!* A lifetime of hard work learning Torah and working on one's personality will constantly release, bring to consciousness, innate wisdom. Often when one hears something beautiful and true one has the sensation, not of learning something, but of *recognizing* something! A sensitive individual will feel intimations of his or her own deep intuitive level often.

The pathway is clear — a person is born with a lifetime of work ahead, spiritual wisdom and growth are hard-earned. *But the inspiration is within;* you were once there! And that inner sense of inspiration provides the motivation, the source of optimism and confidence that genuine achievement is possible, even assured, if the necessary effort is made.[*]

---

[*] This also gives an insight into how a person can generate a *chiddush* (novel idea) in Torah. How can a human being originate Torah? Torah is a gift from a higher dimension, surely. But the answer is clear: a human being can bring original, genuine Torah into

*   *   *

A second application: a characteristic feature of childhood, and relatively, of the teenage years, is inspired optimism and the lack of a sense of limitation. Children believe that they can become anything. The world is larger-than-life to a child, a child is not oppressed by a limited sense of what is possible. A child has simply to be exposed to almost any form of greatness (unfortunately, all too often physical and meaningless) to begin fantasizing about becoming or achieving that same thing.

However, later in life one is lucky to have any inspiration left at all. Many adults wonder why life seemed so rich when they were teenagers, why they could laugh or cry so richly, so fully, back then; and why life seems so flat (at best) now. But the idea is as we have described above. First comes a phase of *unreal* positivity, a charge of energy. And then life challenges one to climb back to real achievement independently.

*   *   *

A third application is to be found in the *ba'al teshuva* world (*ba'al teshuva* describes a person who has discovered a Torah-oriented way of life after living a more secular lifestyle). Many *ba'alei teshuva* experience an unexpected and disturbing letdown. Often the pathway is as follows. A young person discovers Torah, becomes inspired by a Torah teacher, and begins to study. Every Torah experience, whether in learning or in contact with the Orthodox world, is spectacular. Every text

---

the world because it is contained within him already, at a level deeper than the conscious. All that is needed is to lower a bucket into the deep well of the *neshama* (soul) and draw that wisdom!

studied is alive with significance, every Shabbos experience is high, and there is a phase of euphoria. Somehow though, subtly, this changes and growth has to be sought. Learning may be very difficult. Often the difficulties seem to far outweigh the breakthroughs. Many are tempted not to persevere in learning. Of course this is exactly the way it must be, real growth in learning comes when real effort is generated. Just as physical muscle is built only against strenuous resistance, so too spiritual and personality growth is built only against equivalent resistance. A person who understands this secret can begin to *enjoy* the phase of work; a maturity of understanding makes clear that the first phase was artificial, it is the second phase which yields real development.

* * *

Perhaps the sharpest application of this idea in modern Western society is in marriage. Marriage today is to a large extent in ruins in the secular world. In many communities divorce is more usual than survival of marriage, and even in those marriages which do survive it is common to find much disharmony.

One of the prime factors in this disastrous situation is the lack of understanding of our subject. Marriage has two distinct phases: romance, and love. Romance is the initial, heady, illogical swirl of emotion which characterizes a new relationship and it can be extreme. Love, in Torah terms, is the result of much genuine giving. Love is generated essentially not by what one receives from a partner, but by the well-utilized opportunity to give, and to give *oneself*. The phase of romance very soon fades, in fact just as soon as it is grasped it begins to die. A spiritually sensitive person knows that this must be so, but instead of becoming depressed and concerned that one has married the wrong person, one should realize that the phase of work, of giving, is just beginning. The phase of building real love can now flourish. In fact, in Hebrew there is no word for "romance" — in its depth it is an illusion. However, in the world of secular values, the first flash, the "quick fix", is everything. "Love" is translated as "romance" and when it dies, what is left? No-one has taught young people that love and life are about giving and building, and so the tendency is to give up and search for a "quick fix" elsewhere. Of course, the search *must* fail because no new experience will last. Understanding this well can make the difference between marital misery or worse and a lifetime of married happiness. Jewish marriage is carefully crafted to transition from initial inspiration, not to disappointment but to even deeper inspiration. The menstrual separation laws are just one example — instead of allowing intensity to dull into tired familiarity, phases of separation generate new inspiration and the magic never fades.

*   *   *

In all these applications, and in fact in all of life, the challenge of the second phase is to remember the first, to remain inspired by that memory and to use it as fuel for constant growth. The Rambam describes life as a dark night on a stormy plain — lashed by the rain, lost in the darkness, one is faced with despair. Suddenly, there is a flash of lightning. In a millisecond the scenery is as clear as day, one's direction obvious. But just as soon as it is perceived it disappears; and one must fight on through the storm with only the memory of that flash for guidance. The lightning lasts very briefly; the darkness may seem endless.

That is the pattern of life, short-lived inspiration and lengthy battles. The tools needed are determination, perseverance and a stubborn refusal to despair. Personal ordeals which make despair seem imminent are in reality a father's hands, withdrawn so that you can learn to walk. And the work of remembering the flash of light when it seems impossible is *emuna*, faith.

The third phase, and happy is the one who attains it while yet alive, is transcendence. It is a regaining of the level of the first phase, but now deserved, earned, and therefore far beyond it.

There is a statement of the Sages which describes the final transcendence, the transition from this world to the next, and it describes the angels which come to greet a person at that time. One of these angels comes to search out "Where is this person's Torah, and is it complete in his hand." The Gaon of Vilna points out, chillingly, that the higher being which asks this question is not a stranger. Suddenly one recognizes the very same angel with whom he learned Torah in the womb! And the question to be answered is: Where is that Torah which inspired you then? Have you brought it into the world and made it real? And can it now be called yours?

Chapter 3

Laughter

L et us look more closely at the transition from ordeal to deliverance. A most illuminating way to approach this subject is to understand the deeper meaning of laughter, for the mystical concept is that the response to deliverance from imminent disaster is the root of laughter.

To understand this we shall have to note a basic premise: the physical world is constructed on a root dimension of deeper forces. Everything in the world reflects its root in a higher level exactly. That is how we can have access to understanding the spiritual world: although we have no sense organs to apprehend it directly, we can grasp the nature of the physical world and then translate its structure, in every detail, to an understanding of the spiritual world. In fact, the only path to the spiritual is through the medium of the physical. Perhaps the most potent illustration of this idea lies in understanding the manner in which we relate to another human being. When someone does or says something significant or meaningful and you respond inwardly, emotionally, what you are conscious of is the appreciation of that person's attitude or feeling towards you and its effect on your relationship. What you are *not* conscious of is that person's lips moving or muscles twitching, which in fact is exactly what is happening in the physical world. In other words, we automatically translate the vehicle of the physical into its deeper meaning. One can access another person's mind or personality *only* by means of the physical vehicle of their body, and yet that access is achieved effortlessly and naturally.

The skill of spiritual living, of course, is to use that subtle and powerful "switching mechanism" always, in relation to everything in the physical world, and to inwardly perceive the deeper level and meaning behind all the world's objects and phenomena.

So if we wish to grasp a spiritual idea we must analyze its expression in the physical. What is the nature of laughter in the physical world? What exactly provokes the universal human response of laughter?

*   *   *

An examination of human laughter will show that what causes us to laugh is a sharp and improbable juxtaposition of opposites. When a process moves in one direction and then suddenly and unexpectedly changes to its opposite, laughter is generated. In fact, the more extreme the contrast, the more extreme the tension before the reversal and the more sudden the snap into reversal, the more intense the laughter. Strangely, this is true even when the events or processes observed are *not intrinsically funny* at all: laughter at the plight of the victim of a practical joke is highly incongruous and yet may be almost unavoidable — why is this so? The spectacle of a pompous, conceited individual strutting along in overbearing self-confidence laid low by a mere banana peel is not at all humorous, and yet even those rushing to help may not be able to hide a smile; what is the meaning of this strange phenomenon?

The idea here is as follows. Real, spiritual laughter is the cosmic response to a real change. We find this expressed in p'sukim (verses): "Az yemalei s'chok pinu — Then our mouths shall be filled with laughter"; "then" but not now. In fact according to halacha we may not laugh with complete abandon in this phase of the world's history while the pain of exile is still with us; but during and after the transition to redemption full laughter will be appropriate. And amazingly: "Va'tischak le'yom acharon"; a woman of valor will "laugh at the last day" — imagine laughing at the day of death! But of course the transition into eternal life, when that reality is revealed, is the happiest event imaginable! A woman who is "of valor", correctly prepared in spiritual strength, will certainly feel that simcha (joy); and particularly a woman, since she has just that greatness of spirit which enables her to be a vehicle of birth, she can most deeply understand the happiness of potential life becoming actual.

*   *   *

Let us look deeper. In the spiritual path, what is the change which generates the exhilaration of spiritual laughter? It is the change from ordeal to redemption; and more specifically, from intense crisis to seemingly impossible redemption. When crisis leaves no option but total despair and at that point deliverance occurs, laughter is the result. When Avraham and Sarah give birth to the first child born into the line of the Jewish people, we are taught this secret. Avraham was extremely old. Sarah was far beyond child-bearing age. The *gemara* says that she was intrinsically infertile — *she had no womb*. When these two people, totally devoid of any possibility of having a child, were told that they would in fact have a child, *they laughed*. And a child was born. And his Divinely-given name was Yitzchak — "He shall laugh". And is that not the entire story of the Jewish people? *We begin where the impossible ends.*

When Yitzchak grows up, he is sacrificed by his father. Sacrificed, and not sacrificed. In physical terms, he is saved and climbs down from the altar. But the deeper wisdom states "The ashes of Yitzchak are laid out before Me" — in spiritual terms he is sacrificed. One aspect of the meaning of this paradox is that Yitzchak subsequently lives in two worlds: physically here but spiritually transcendent. And the mystics again refer to his name: the word Yitzchak יצחק comprises קץ חי — "death in life", or better, "the next world while yet alive". The man whose name means laughter (and "name" always denotes essence in Torah) spans two worlds; he lives in the world of ordeal, of challenge, and has about him an aura of the world of deliverance. Is that not, indeed, the story of the Jewish people?

*   *   *

The Rambam explains that the birth of a child is a microcosm of this idea. The mystery and miracle of human birth powerfully reveal the forces of intense reversal which takes place at the interface between two worlds. The experience of the mother is perhaps the clearest example of the pathway of ordeal to redemption. Pregnancy proceeds gradually and predictably. Then, like most ordeals and crises, labor occurs abruptly and is incomparable in intensity relative to the preceding months. Labor certainly does not seem to be a life-giving experience — if one who had no knowledge of human physiology and birth witnessed labor for the first time he would be convinced that a disaster was taking place. At the height of the labor, when superficially all looks worst, a child is born. And only then does it become apparent that the entire process was birth, not the opposite.

But more deeply, the experience of the child teaches our principle. The unborn child lives in a medium in which it is perfectly adapted — submerged in liquid, with a blood circulation and other details of its physiology specific to its intra-uterine environment. Its lungs are collapsed and non-functional, blood bypasses the lungs, the heart has openings between its chambers unlike an adult heart; in short, many of its features are radically different from those of a person already born. But more than this, those features are life-sustaining in that environment and would be lethal in this one, and the features which are needed to sustain life here would be lethal there: truly a situation of opposites.

Then birth begins: a child perfectly adapted to one set of conditions is thrust into another set where death must be only minutes away — this child has only the opposite of what it needs to survive! And miraculously, within a few critical minutes, *everything reverses!* "What is closed opens, and what is open closes", states the *gemara*. Almost instantaneously the lungs open and breathe, blood is simultaneously routed to the lungs, blood pouring out of the umbilical vessels is mysteriously arrested as those vessels powerfully constrict, and suddenly a child is alive in this world and perfectly adapted to it!

Birth is the symbol of all transitions, and it teaches us to be sensitive in understanding them. The Rambam quotes this phenomenon to illustrate a firm root for our faith that there is a transition from this world to the next: although on this side of the great divide we perceive only a change from life to death, we can begin to understand more deeply that fundamental of faith, that death leads, in fact, to life — on the far side of that divide, the reversals miraculously begin. *"Va'tischak le'yom acharon* — She laughs at the last day".

* * *

If this is true for personal crisis, it is true for the Jewish people too. We were formed in the crucible of Egyptian slavery. The root of that ordeal, however, was the experience of Yosef and his brothers in Egypt previously; the deeds and experiences of the sons are presaged by those of the fathers. An examination of the course of events which brought the sons of Yaakov to face their brother Yosef in Egypt will teach us all the features of ordeals and crises, both personal and national.

The brothers made a mistake — they sold Yosef. The root of trials, often hidden, begins with human error. (One who wishes can trace this entire process in its own root — the experience of Adam and all subsequent human history.) And that is when an agonizing ordeal began for them. When they returned to their father with the evidence of Yosef's fate, Yaakov lost his prophetic insight in mourning. The brothers witnessed their father lose his direct connection with the spiritual world, and they knew that they were the cause. Then, like many ordeals, the torment became prolonged — they did not see the resolution of their mistake for many years; it was over twenty years later that they met Yosef again. During those years they watched their father mourn in the intensity of acute mourning for one newly lost; his emotion never abated. It must have seemed to them that they had been the cause of permanently obstructing the destiny of the Jewish people, and hence of the entire Universe; we can only imagine their suffering.

This is the classic pathway of human difficulty — an ordeal begins, and then seems endless. Its very duration seems to preclude redemption. And then it intensifies to levels which previously would have seemed impossible to survive — ordeal becomes crisis. And the crisis gets worse: the brothers travel to Egypt in search of food. Instead of obtaining food with no hindrance, they find themselves accused of spying by a man who becomes their tormentor (Yosef, of course, unknown to them). Eventually they return to Canaan with food but leaving one of their number behind as ransom to force them to bring Binyamin (Benjamin) down to Egypt later. And we learn yet another feature of human difficulty — it often seems so unintelligible, so unfair, in fact such a nightmare. They discover their money returned — more confusion, and they return to their father.

Of course, as we witness events unfolding, we begin to understand what they cannot. Yosef is torturing them *in order to bring about their redemption,* for their good, motivated only by love for them. He wants them to bring Binyamin, another son of Rachel, just as he is, down to him so that he can place them in a crossfire of loyalty, tempt them to betray and reject Binyamin in circumstances similar to those in which they had failed so many years before with him, and this time to *get it right,* to correct their original mistake in full *teshuva* (repentance). And thereby to return cosmic history to its course. The ultimate stakes are involved. He cannot reveal himself to them, he must suffer as they suffer, he must be outwardly cruel to redeem them. The message we are being taught is obvious — *suffering has a purpose*, a specific purpose, and even though it hurts like fire and seems impossible to understand, the Master of the Universe is engineering redemption and yes, somehow suffering with His people, individually and collectively.

Finally, the famine leaves Yaakov and the brothers with no food. He has no option but to part with Binyamin. They take Binyamin down to Egypt and then, perhaps most cruel of all, things seem to be fine — they are all released, homeward bound with food, all together, intact. Very often, final crisis is preceded by an illusion of salvation. Euphoria develops, the relief is tangible; and then unprecedented disaster arrives.* As they travel, hoofbeats are heard behind them — Yosef has sent a messenger to search their belongings, he has been robbed. The stolen object is found in Binyamin's sack. The brothers face the ultimate temptation (and how ready we often are to accept the facts at face value and clinch destruction ourselves) — not only has Binyamin been given gifts by the Egyptian ruler in their presence (to tempt them into jealousy of him as they were jealous of Yosef long before) but now they have *evidence* that he is the cause of their predicament! And yet they come through, they stand by him, they redeem themselves by placing loyalty above their subjective judgement and emotions.

---

* Generations later, when Moshe Rabbeinu (Moses) enters the palace of Pharaoh and the Jewish people await seemingly imminent release — can we imagine the bitter test of faith they experience when their redeemer returns from Pharaoh and they discover that not only is the slavery to continue, but they now have to produce the same amount of bricks daily — without straw!

They return to Egypt for the showdown. As they face Yosef, the only options are all destruction. Either they return to Canaan, to face their father without Binyamin as Yosef demands and thereby kill Yaakov (the commentaries point out that Yaakov would have died of grief instantaneously upon seeing them without Binyamin); or destroy Egypt. The *midrashim* are clear that Yehuda (Judah) instructed his brothers that they were to literally destroy Egypt, the empire of the entire known world at the time (all the Patriarchs were of superhuman strength). Either option, total destruction.

Yehuda steps forward and faces his tormentor. The brothers had long previously realized that they were being subjected to this agonizing sequence because of their sin, but they were here about to expiate it fully. In that moment of confused agony, on the brink of certain oblivion Yehuda, as the leader, offers himself. He asks Yosef to take him instead of Binyamin, the ultimate act of loyalty and of correcting the root mistake.

At that moment, the brothers hear the words "I am Yosef". Through the haze of agony on the edge of disintegration — "I am Yosef". That is the nature of deliverance — preceded by a yielding of the self; occurring at the impossible moment, and most strikingly: spoken by the source of the torment! The cause of the problem, the Egyptian persecutor, is revealed as the source of redemption, Yosef their brother.

*   *   *

We can note two elements in this process of revelation of redemption, one deeply inspiring and comforting and one sobering. Firstly: a very deep and central concept here is that the redemption is not simply the ending of the pain of ordeal, the release and relief felt on waking from terror. On the contrary, the ordeal itself, the suffering itself, *becomes* the redemption. This must be understood. *Everything* Hashem does is good, not just the ending. In the indescribable emotions the brothers must have felt when they realized they were facing Yosef was the understanding that what they had been through was essential, life-saving. They could appreciate every detail of the torment they had experienced as intrinsic to their happiness now, for without it they would not have achieved perfection. Now, in retrospect, they would not sacrifice one moment of their previous suffering! In fact they would savor and cherish each of those moments for the rest of their lives. That is the real joy of redemption, the realization that the ordeal and its resolution are in fact *both* the redemption. The ultimate humor, the ultimate irony is that when the truth is revealed, the problem is the solution.

This idea is expressed in general life terms as follows. There is a mystical statement that in the next world "The taste of the tree and the taste of the fruit are the same". In the world to come, where the abstract image of that dimension is that of a garden of trees, those trees are unusual — not only is the fruit edible, but so are the trees themselves. What is the meaning of this? After our discussion it is not difficult to fathom at least some of the beauty of this concept. "Trees" and "fruit" in Torah allude to the ideas of "process" and "end-result". After all, a this-worldly tree cannot be eaten, but it is a basis for producing fruit, which can. There are always two phases — work and preparation, and then results and reward. The tree is only a means to an end — the fruit. This world is like the tree — it is the place of work and preparation. The next world is like the fruit — sweet and edible and containing seeds for endless growth. But here we learn our secret: in the next world what is revealed is that the tree, too, is in reality part of the end-result. The sweetness of the next world lies not in the fact that the difficulties of this world are finally over, but rather that the difficulties of this world *themselves* are the substance of eternal achievement. We do not aim to get through this world without engaging it in order to achieve reality in the next; it is our fully engaging and grappling with this world itself which *is* our reality in the next. The difference that this view of life and its loads makes is enormous. Although ordeals remain ordeals, and often no more intelligible for this knowledge at all, yet knowing that these trials are the substance of ultimate reality, that this suffering will be one's happiness and exactly what one needs is a deep source of strength.

The second element we note is this. We said that the experience of moving from crisis to redemption causes laughter. The juxtaposition of such extremes, so suddenly, is the root of spiritual laughter and that is the meaning of "*Az ye'malei s'chok pinu* — Then our mouths will be filled with laughter" and "*Va'tischak le'yom acharon* — She laughs at the last day". However when Yosef revealed himself to his brothers, it does not state that they laughed. Quite the contrary, their shock was extreme. Let us understand this.

When someone goes through a sudden reversal of state, when a false state of being in the personality is reversed, or to put it in extreme terms when the practical joke is played, the humor of the situation is obvious — *but only to the onlookers*. The one who is experiencing this sudden change does not see the humor at all. The shock of being forced to admit, of being brought face to face with one's false image, one's dearly-held but wrong convictions, one's imperfect personality structure, is no laughing matter. And if those brothers, men of consummate spiritual greatness who had just now corrected their personal error, were shocked at the revelation of truth — how will we feel? When this world is turned upside-down at the redemption, the joke will be on those who must themselves be turned upside-down. Jewish living therefore, is an attempt to live in opposition to the secular values of the world: if you like, to live upside-down here. When that final and massive inversion occurs, we would like to find ourselves already upright and able to witness the correction of values without needing the shock of experiencing it in our flesh.

* * *

These two elements always apply. In the mystical root there is an idea that Hashem Himself laughs, as it were. "*Yoshev ba'shamayim yischak, Hashem yil'ag lamo*— He who sits in Heaven shall laugh, Hashem shall mock them (the wicked)". Hashem's laughter is directed at the fact that as evil intensifies, it generates its own annihilation. Hashem's *hashgacha* (management of the world's affairs) so arranges things that all the evil machinations of the wicked rebound on themselves, an irony which mocks them in the deepest sense. Their negative actions turn out to be the source of their own destruction, and in spiritual terms this is the highest humor. While Pharaoh is desperately trying to destroy Jewish children so that the redeemer who has been foretold should not live beyond childhood, he is himself unwittingly raising that redeemer in his own household.

When Haman builds gallows for Mordechai, he is hanged on those gallows himself. The forces he unleashes to destroy the

Jewish people are themselves used to save them and destroy their enemies. In fact, at the heart of the message of Purim is *"v'nahafoch hu* — And it was overturned", or reversed. *"Hipuch"*, total inversion, is the Purim story. All the darkness of the Persian experience is manifest: Hashem's name is not mentioned in the *megilla*, "Esther" *means* "hidden", even the fate of the Jews is sealed by pure "chance" — the drawing of lots. And all that changes to light, Hashem's name is surely revealed, and the very lots that fall out on Moshe Rabbeinu's *yahrzeit* (date of death) also "happen" to indicate his day of birth. The very same things, but their very opposite. That is the message of Purim, the mask and the removal of the mask. That is the laughter of Purim. And we learn that the light of the world, Torah, was ignited on Purim: although the Torah was accepted at Sinai, its deeper and more binding acceptance occurred at Purim. Since Sinai was incandescent with obvious revelation, say the commentaries, the Jewish people were forced to accept Torah — how could they deny? But at Purim, where no revealed miracles took place and the only thing obvious was darkness, they were free to reject it, to refuse to see the Divine hand in natural events. When they accepted Torah then, voluntarily, that was real acceptance; that is a permanent bond with Torah.

Only when there is a possibility of wrong can right be manifest. Only when it is difficult can meaningful progress occur. To expand a famous statement of the Zohar: Only through the darkness of ordeals can the light of personal growth be revealed.

Chapter 4

Ordeal and Miracle

L et us focus on the subject of the purpose of ordeals and the personality tools needed to deal with them successfully.

The Mesillas Yesharim says that the purpose of life is "to perform *mitzvos*, to serve, and to *withstand tests*". Now a classic question is asked here: why are we tested? Why would Hashem test us, since He knows beforehand what the outcome must be? If ordeals are "tests", as נסיון *nisayon*, is often translated, the purpose of these tests cannot be for Hashem's learning anything about us, of course. Then who benefits? And how?

To this question we can add another. The word נסיון *nisayon* is based on the root נס meaning a miracle. (נס also means a banner, a flag raised high: a miracle is really a banner clearly marking Hashem's presence in the world.) The problem is, what do ordeals have to do with the miraculous? Exactly which element of a test is miraculous? We can put this question most sharply as follows: when one is faced with an ordeal, can one overcome it? In principle, is it possible to overcome ordeals or not? If it is possible, where is the *miracle* in succeeding? And of course, if it is not possible, why would Hashem demand the impossible of us?

* * *

Before we examine this question along the lines which we have been following, let us understand one of the answers usually given. There is an idea that a test forces one to discover levels of one's own inner strength which were previously hidden. The difficulty of the test brings out that which would have remained dormant without it. It is not Hashem who discovers what you are capable of when you succeed, it is you! Mystically, the concept here is that of bringing the potential into the actual; before the test there was a level of power in the personality which was potential only, after the test that power has become actual, realized in the personality and in the world. For Avraham Avinu to be *able* to sacrifice his son is not enough — he must make that ability an action, he must bring it into the world. What counts, in other words, is not what one can do, but what one actually does in life.

There are deep correlates of this idea: the *neshama* (soul) itself is, in a sense, potential, and the mystical understanding is that a *neshama* without a body cannot effect any change, it must be brought into a body, into the finite, tangible world in order to achieve — potential energy is not enough, action is necessary. Even deeper, we note that Hashem Himself found it necessary to create a world — being able to do so was not enough for Him; He thereby demonstrates to us most powerfully that potential must be made concrete, crystallized into tangible reality.

While this approach is certainly true, it does not answer the specific question with which we began: where is the miracle? If the potential was present, and was simply revealed by the test, that is not miraculous.

The *gemara* contains a fascinating insight into this problem. In explaining the background to David Hamelech's relationship with Batsheva and the sin he committed, the *gemara* records the following conversation between David and the Creator. David asks "Hashem, why do we say Elokei Avraham (the G-d of Abraham), Elokei Yitzchak (the G-d of Isaac) and Elokei Yaakov (the G-d of Jacob), but we do not say Elokei David (the G-d of David)?"

Let us understand this question. David was certainly not asking in pride. He was a true servant of Hashem who had virtually conquered pride entirely; in fact mystically David represents the power of *malchus*, kingship, which means a revelation of Hashem's kingship in the world — the Jewish king is simply the agent who makes Hashem's rule apparent. The *mashiach* is to be descended from David and an extension of his person and *neshama*, and his purpose will be to bring about a recognition of Divine rule, certainly not human rule. The deeper wisdom describes the attribute of the *mashiach* and Jewish kingship as *"leis lei mi'garmei klum* — he has nothing of his own". David was asking in utter humility. David, who so intensely embodied this virtue, wanted to know where his service of Hashem fell short: Avraham, Yitzchak and Yaakov merit to have their names mentioned together with the Divine, in other words, they reveal Hashem's presence by their lives; and David, the fourth mystical corner of the Divine chariot, does not. If all four of them are to function together, as they must eventually, David wanted to know what element of his life had not yet been adequately developed.

Hashem answers: "They were tested by Me, and you have not been tested." Immediately David answers "Hashem, grant me a test!" He is granted a test, and he fails.

If we analyze these lines of *gemara* we are forced to a startling conclusion: the result of being tested and succeeding, it seems, is that Hashem's name can be attached to the name of the one who is tested. What does this mean?

* * *

A name is a revelation of essence. If a person's name, revealing his essence, is spoken together with Hashem's name, the idea is that an aspect of Hashem's presence is revealed in that person; that individual has somehow become a vehicle for Hashem's manifestation in the world. When Avraham Avinu is tested in the fire of the *akeida* (binding and sacrifice of Yitzchak) Hashem is revealed. How does this happen?

The answer is that a real test is *impossible*. It stresses a person beyond all possible limits. The feeling of the enormity of a real ordeal is accurate: *this test is too much for me!* When a person faces the impossible chasm, and leaps anyway because Hashem asks it, and *miraculously* arrives on the other side, Hashem is revealed because only He can do the impossible — *that* is the miracle! The banner of miracle, of Divine imminence, has been raised. Two elements are required: to attach oneself to the Divine; and then to leap. The Sages tell us that a person's own lower self (*yetzer hara*) attacks him daily with lethal viciousness, (the essence of all tests), and "if Hashem does not help, one *cannot* overcome it"! There are no inaccuracies in the statements of our Sages — if they tell us that without Divine assistance the battle is impossible, so it must be. So that to perceive victory in ordeals is to perceive the Divine hand!

When a person acts beyond the level of normal, expected human action, Hashem is revealed. The *gemara* records that Shimon ben Shetach, the great scholar and sage, once bought a donkey from a gentile and discovered a precious jewel attached to it. He returned the jewel to its owner, explaining that he had paid for a donkey, not a jewel. The gentile exclaimed "Baruch Elokei Shimon ben Shetach — Blessed is the G-d of Shimon ben Shetach!" That response so clearly expresses exactly what we have learned: not "Blessed is Shimon ben Shetach" but "Blessed is *the G-d of* Shimon ben Shetach" — Hashem's name together with his! The gentile appreciated immediately that when a human acts against human nature he is expressing a connection with a higher reality — a small miracle has occurred!

We see this in many ways. The Mesillas Yesharim, when dealing with the higher levels which a person can reach, says "*t'chillaso avoda, ve'sofo g'mul* — the beginning is work but the end is a gift". The beginning of the path which leads to transcendence is hard work, very hard work, but the end is a gift, it comes from elsewhere, from beyond the work, beyond the self. The Sages say that if a person states that he "labored and found" (יגעתי ומצאתי) he is to be believed. Labor will lead to results; but the words are so potently clear: the word "found" connotes an *unexpected* find (מציאה); it does not say "labored and achieved" but rather "labored and found" — the find was unexpected, a surprise *despite* the work because it so completely belongs to another dimension.

The prayer of one who stands tested, therefore is "Hashem, this test that You have given me seems impossible to me. I cannot humanly overcome it. But if You have seen fit to test me thus, I shall go through the impossible for You. I shall leap; I give myself to You. I acknowledge that I am nothing, You are everything. Help me through."

* * *

Let us apply this idea. The *akeida* (binding of Yitzchak): the commentaries explain just how impossible Avraham's test was — to sacrifice a son for whom he had waited into extreme old age, from whom he foresaw the Jewish people descending; after teaching the world that human sacrifice is wrong; a man whose entire personality was kindness and love. And not just to harm that son in some minor way, but to kill him with his own hand. Beyond the emotional level, the intellectual level was no less difficult — it made no sense. Hashem had promised him progeny from Yitzchak — how could there be a contradiction in the Divine? But the mystical level expresses an even deeper problem: Avraham *knew* that Hashem *did not want* this sacrifice (as the verse states:"*V'lo alsa al libi* — Which I never intended") as one knows the mind of the beloved — and he was correct; in fact ultimately Hashem prevented him from carrying it out! So he had all levels of his consciousness crying out that this action could not be done, and Hashem said to him, in effect, "Yes, all that you feel and know is true, but kill him anyway"! *That* is a test! *That* is facing the impossible! And Avraham proceeded to do the impossible.

The result? The impossible occurred, the miraculous manifested. We are told in *Chumash* that Yitzchak was spared, he climbed down off the altar, and a ram was offered in his stead. But we are told in the *midrash: "Efro shel Yitzchak munach le'fanai* — the ashes of Yitzchak lie before Me": in a higher dimension, he *was* sacrificed! Not the "ashes of the ram" but the "ashes of Yitzchak". He became an *"olah temimah"* a pure burnt offering. The impossible paradox — a man who lives physically in this world, but spiritually in the next, *simultaneously!* And the qualities of father and son live on in the Jewish people — the ability to yield the emotions, the intellect, the entire personality to Hashem in *emuna* (faith), and the gift of being able to live in a physical world and transcend it at the same time. They leave us the legacy of having to live this way, being forced by test after test to climb, to elevate the material to the spiritual and survive, miraculously.

What of David and Batsheva? The *gemara* searches for an understanding of exactly where David sinned. The simple meaning of the words may be misleading — the *gemara* states that there was no sin of adultery or any other lowly error which may be read into the words. In fact Batsheva was destined for him, and from them was born Shlomo (Solomon) the direct forebear of the *mashiach*. The conclusion of the *gemara* is that David's error was that he *asked to be tested!* This needs understanding. What is wrong with asking for a test? If the purpose of life is to be tested, why should we not actively seek ordeals? But the answer lies in the very question. When one asks for a test one is asserting the confidence that one can succeed in the test: "Test me — I'll show you!" No-one asks for a test which he is certain to fail!

And that confidence, that ego, that element of pride is just what *nisayon* (test) comes to neutralize, to eliminate. When David asked to be tested, he manifested an infinitesimal degree of pride, at his supernal level. And the work which he is destined to do in the world is to show that he is nothing, that

Hashem is everything, *"leis lei mi'garmei klum"*. Hashem carries us through. We act, but He accomplishes. For the man who is to teach this most powerfully to the Jewish people and the world even the smallest degree of asserting that he can do something independently of Hashem, as it were, is too much. Even though he had emptied himself of almost all vested interest, all ego, yet that tiny speck of pride was too much. And the only possible result, the solution in fact, was to fail; failure is the correction of the ego. David's success was not yet to be; that fourth element of the Divine chariot will be manifest, in fact, through him at the end of time.

*　　*　　*

We learn an exhilarating depth here. Ordeal leads to transcendence. In the paradox of facing crisis with a lion's strength and yet inwardly knowing that only Hashem manifests here, we reveal Him openly. What is possible and what is impossible is not our concern. The Alter of Kelm used to say "Ask not if a thing is possible, ask only if it is necessary." Our concern is to rise to that partnership with the Divine which invites Him, as it were, to reach down to us.

Chapter 5

Doubt and Certainty

A close examination of human difficulties will reveal that at their root lies doubt. Not knowing with full confidence what one's direction should be is the most energy-sapping element in our lives. In depth, all our existential tension and anxiety stem from doubt. In isolated ordeals and in life in general we struggle most profoundly to identify the correct path — and it seems impossible. Very often the problem lies not in finding the strength to cope with adversity — one feels one would go through fire willingly if only one knew in which direction! If only we could be sure that this or that particular path were correct in an absolute sense, that it would not let us down unpredictably, we would find the raw courage to walk that path. But that is not our experience: we choose a direction, perhaps feeling that this must be the correct one, and tomorrow we are forced to wonder how we could possibly have seen things that way yesterday — the situation appears exactly opposite now. And of course, the next day we feel even more confused — eventually we lose confidence in our sense of direction altogether. Life is a halting, faltering business — three steps ahead today, two backwards tomorrow, and so often no more than helpless circles with the dismay of crossing our own tracks repeatedly.

Let us dissect this matter. The mystics call this world *"alma d'sfeika"* — a world of doubt. Intrinsically, the world is a confusing mixture of good and bad, true and false. It is also called *"alma d'shikra"* — a world of falsehood; however the deepest essence of that falsehood is that it contains an admixture of good: if not for the component of good it could never exist, and therein lies the confusion. In fact, the most dangerous forms of falsehood are those which contain *almost* all truth — they are the most deceptive. Nothing in the world is entirely good or bad, every choice, every decision has a cost, and in many ordeals the combination of factors on either side of the moral choice is so complex that we respond with paralysis.

* * *

What is the source of doubt underlying this *"alma d'sfeika"*? The answer of course, must be in Torah, in the Torah's description of how the human condition came to be what it is. Adam Harishon (Adam) was faced with the primal choice — to obey the Divine command and refrain from eating the fruit of the "tree of the knowledge of good and evil" or to disobey. The world he experienced was perfect; the tree however, held the awesome power to loose evil into the world.

A striking question which must be asked is: why is the tree referred to as "the tree of the knowledge of *good and evil*"? Surely it should be named "the tree of the knowledge of *evil*"; it is the source of evil in the Creation, why *good and* evil? But that is the point exactly. If the tree were of evil only, that evil would be so easily identifiable, so odious and hideous that no-one would ever engage it! It would be the most obvious thing in the world to avoid — it would never present a temptation, an ordeal. It is the knowledge of good and evil *combined,* confused, which is the problem! "Knowledge" (*da'as*) always means intimate association, intrinsic bonding: the tree combines good and evil so thoroughly that after its fruit is ingested the human becomes a tangled knot of both elements. No situation is entirely clear thereafter. Never can we completely separate our lower selves, our vested interests, from our pure core dimension. And *that* is the problem.

That is the root of all sadness. The Hebrew word for "weeping" is בכי from the root meaning to be lost in confusion (מבוכה). The word for a "tear", the eye's issue in weeping, is דמעה from a root meaning a mixture of the pure and the profane (דמע).

When Adam confronted that tree, he was pure and the world was pure. Evil existed only as an objective, dispassionate possibility external to himself. But when he ate that fruit evil became internalized within himself and within the goodness of the world and now the human mind can never resolve its doubts entirely, never read the world plainly as the open book it once was. No wonder the mystics refer to the tree of the knowledge of good and evil as *"ilana d'sfeika"* — the tree of doubt!

*　　*　　*

What happens after man eats from the tree? He hides in the

garden. Hides from Hashem, Who is everywhere! How could Adam imagine that he could hide — he knew Hashem as no human has ever since, knew deeply that Hashem is all-seeing and all-knowing? How could he hope to escape by hiding? The answer is that he no longer sees reality clearly — on the one hand he knows Hashem exists, that is why he is hiding! But on the other hand, he somehow thinks, incredibly, that he can hide! What a most deeply pathetic figure he has become, hiding from that which he knows is inescapable and yet fooling himself anyway. Is that not the description of our lives?

And far more shocking, Hashem's response. Hashem appears in the garden and calls to Adam "Where are you?" The Creator of the Universe, Who sees all, knows all, asks "Where are you?" *As if* He cannot see Adam! When man attempts to hide, to blur reality into a crazy, fractured version of itself, Hashem responds in kind, *allows* man to see the world that way; measure for measure exactly. You wish to escape My notice, to feel you are independent, hidden from My gaze? *"Where are you?"* Man is allowed to perceive falsely that he is alone — the greatest pain of all.

The Jewish people's arch-rival is the nation of Amalek. The numerical value of עמלק "Amalek" and of ספק *"safek"* (doubt) is identical. The descendant of Amalek who tried to destroy the entire Jewish people was Haman: the *gemara* indicates his name in the garden of Eden, at the time of Adam's sin; when Hashem asks Adam that second question "Did you eat from the tree? — *Hamin ha'etz"* the word *"hamin"* ("Did you?") is the name "Haman". That gap between reality and perception, the gap of doubt, opens with the sin. And that is our enemy.

After his expulsion from the garden, Adam cannot go back. Placed as guards outside the garden are Beings wielding swords.

The swords are unusual — they flash blades turning continually: *"es lahav ha' cherev ha' mis' hapeches* — the blade of the turning sword". There are commentaries who explain this symbolism: the turning sword is the lethal weapon of doubt. Today one's reality appears thus and tomorrow different. Always. And man cannot find the road back to the garden — the garden keeps eluding him, the road keeps changing. Not only is he confused about where he is, but the road back to clarity is in doubt too.

* * *

Admixture is a part of our world. The mystics say that just as Adam ingested a mixture, so we are condemned to do the same in our very bodies — our food is a mixture of wholesomeness and waste. Together they are tasty; but within the body the necessary elements are extracted and absorbed and the waste is revealed as offensive in the extreme. *Within* the organism of our being! When people reach spiritual purity — when some element of the garden is attained — this ceases: in the desert the Jewish people ate manna, and there was no excretion. Pure existence can be fed by pure food, and there is no waste, no lower side of reality, and no need for separation. Of course that generation's counterpart was the cult of Pe'or — the worship of excretion and excrement. This is obvious. The evil forces work to focus on the lower, the impure, and to present them as worthy of worship. In fact, in Torah all idolatry is referred to as *"avodas gilulim"* — literally the worship of dung. How great will the stench be when the good finally separates permanently from the bad and leaves it to decompose.

Our condition requires a lifetime of separating good from

bad, extracting the pure, the spiritual, the good, and ejecting the evil, exposed for what it is. Our life's work is to strive for this clarity. Everything needs to be examined for its element of *kedusha*, holiness, and that holiness extracted. The verse states *"va'ani esbol va'amalet"* — Hashem Himself says "And I shall bear, and I shall expel" — forcibly eject the evil eventually.

* * *

A fascinating insight into the subject of doubt can be gained from examining the root words themselves, as always in Torah. The Hebrew word for "doubt" is *safek,* and for "certainty" *vadai.* Amazingly, these commonly-used words are not to be found in *Tanach* (the entire Biblical writings)! Nowhere does the Torah mention the words *safek* or *vadai.* Both these words are of Rabbinic origin. Now we know that the essence of an idea is contained in the Torah word for that idea; if there is no word, it surely means that *in essence that concept does not exist.* And of course — the world as formed by its root in Torah *contains no doubt:* things either exist or they do not, there is nothing in the world that exists "doubtfully", tentatively; doubt is *our* problem, a feature of *our perception,* not an objective reality! And if there is no doubt external to us, of course there is no certainty — certainty exists only where doubt is a possibility; if there can be no doubt there can be no certainty, a thing simply "is"!

(The truth is, we are so confused that we say we are sure *exactly* when we are not: "I'm *sure* I saw him yesterday" really means one is not sure at all! When one is certain one simply states the fact: "I saw him yesterday".)

The primal, pristine world of Hashem's Creation is clear and open. We opacify and confuse it. The word for "doubt" is of human origin; it is a result of the damage we do to our own perception.

Doubt is truly brought into being by us. And we must fight our way towards certainty. As we develop our consciousness in spiritual terms we can approach it. On Rosh Hashana and Yom Kippur, when we struggle for ultimate clarity, we say *"ha'vadai shmo, kein tehillaso* — Hashem's name is 'certainty', so be His praise"; the name we attach to Hashem, as it were, in our struggle to see Him more clearly, is *vadai,* certainty. The word for "certainty" too, is of human origin; our battle is to crystallize perception, to make *emes* (truth) shine clearly.

So our ordeals are confusing. That is their essence. Our task is to develop the tenacity to hold onto the truth even when tempted to see it change. Our goal is to break through into clarity — that is transcendence! And that is the meaning of *"Ein simcha k'hataros ha'sfeikos* — There is no happiness like the resolution of doubts". The greatest happiness is simply knowing one's direction. Even if one has not yet started along the road; simply knowing *which* road to follow in life is a great elation. Torah is that direction, and one's *chelek,* one's personal portion in Torah is that road.

Chapter 6

The Root of Evil

If ordeals involve a choice between good and bad, we must examine the nature of the bad. What is the root of evil in the world? How does improper use of free will interact with evil? When Adam chose to eat from the tree, how exactly did evil materialize? And what is the pathway which leads to its correction?

The classical question which can be asked about the realm of evil is: how can evil manifest in a world which is an expression of a Creator Who is good? If Hashem is infinite goodness and the world is no more than an emanation of His being, how can evil arise? We have an axiom that "Evil does not come down from Above".

The question of *why* evil exists in the world is perhaps easier to understand — if the purpose of our existence here is to grapple with moral tests and choose the good, there must be a possibility of choosing the bad. If bad were not a real alternative, we could not be considered free — our correct actions would be inevitable. Of course it follows that if one is not free to do otherwise there can be no credit for doing good. Reward and punishment would be absurd, and life would be a mechanical affair. One who remains at a friend's side when chained there cannot be praised for loyalty — that is compulsion. Therefore evil exists in very real terms and we are entirely free to choose it — so that when we do not, we are performing a meaningful human action. The price we must pay for the privilege of being able to freely choose good is the existence of freely available evil. And the degree of goodness which can be manifest is in direct proportion to the depth of the horror which evil can generate.

But be that as it may, it does not help us understand our question; *how* does evil arise from a source which is pure good? This, the "path of a serpent on a rock" is one of the great mysteries of Creation. Perhaps we can attempt just the beginning of understanding; and to do this we need to study the subject of the *mateh ha'Elokim*, the staff which Moshe Rabbeinu (Moses) carries in his hand.

*   *   *

The more one looks into the nature and the history of this staff, the more amazing and significant it becomes; this is a striking example of something which we tend to regard as unimportant detail, unessential. Of course there is nothing unimportant or unessential in Torah, and if this object features so often at such miraculous events in the Torah narrative it certainly bears intense scrutiny. In the *Chumash* text itself we find the staff in Moshe's hand at the burning bush where it is transformed into a serpent on being thrown to the ground. It appears in Pharaoh's court where it proves to be superior in power to the staffs of the Egyptians. It begins the plagues and splits the sea, and later brings forth water from the rock.

But there is much more. The *midrashim* say that the *mateh* (staff) was made of a sapphire-like material. It was engraved with Hashem's name and also the initials of the ten plagues. (We know that engraving always means that what is engraved is of the essence of the object — not applied *onto* the object as is writing but expressed in the very medium of the object itself.) It began in the possession of Adam at the Creation of the world and was passed down through the generations to Avraham, Yitzchak and Yaakov, and after the generation of the Egyptian exodus, to the kings of Israel. It was held by Pharaoh after Yosef's death and snatched from his palace by Yisro (Jethro) who drove it into the ground outside his home in Midian where no man could extract it until Moshe easily drew it forth — indicating to Yisro his tremendous spiritual power.

If we look more closely we begin to sense something of enormous proportions being hinted at in this easily-overlooked theme of Torah. When Moshe faced the burning bush he was guilty of a slip — he said something inaccurate, inappropriate about the Jewish people, stating that they would not believe him to be the redeemer. In response, when Hashem showed him a sign which he would be able to use to prove his Divine mission to them, that sign took the form of a snake, an unmistakable reference to the sin of slander — it was the primal serpent in the Garden which had misrepresented reality and caused Chava (Eve) to sin. But not just an ordinary snake: Hashem commands Moshe to cast the staff to the ground and it is transformed into a serpent so awesomely terrifying that Moshe flees from it. This needs to be understood: Moshe, the greatest man of all time,

THE ROOT OF EVIL / 61

certainly without mortal fear, and *while speaking to Hashem* which mystically means being completely absorbed in a transcendent state of closeness to Him — *terrified?* How is this possible? We are forced to understand that what confronted him must have been indescribable, cosmic, in its horror. And then he is commanded to grasp it by the tail! He does so, surely an act of unsurpassed self-control, and it instantaneously manifests again as the staff it was originally.

Moshe then performs the same sequence of transformation in the presence of Pharaoh. But the *midrashim* describe seemingly unintelligible events surrounding this scene: when Pharaoh denies knowledge of Hashem, he is shown the *mateh* becoming a serpent. Instead of being duly impressed, he has his magicians do the same with their staffs. Then, cackling like a hen with mirth, says the *midrash*, he calls in his wife who does the same. And then he calls in Egyptian *schoolchildren*, four and five years old, who all cast their staffs to the ground and transform them into serpents! He and his advisors mock Moshe and Aharon, saying that one who has produce to sell usually takes that produce to a market where it is in short supply — you have brought your produce to an overstocked market! Your magic is commonplace here. Moshe cryptically replies that the opposite is true: one who has top-quality produce takes it to a well-stocked market where the dealers are expert so that its quality will stand out against all the inferior goods. Then Aharon's staff swallows up the serpents of the Egyptians *after* becoming a staff again — a double miracle. What does all this mean?

*   *   *

Let us try to perceive more deeply. Firstly, we notice a pervasive duality in the *mateh*. It is engraved with Hashem's name, the name of all-encompassing kindness, but also with the plagues, manifestations of Hashem's strict punitive justice. It is used to perform miracles of salvation and sustenance for the Jewish people, but acts as the rod of retribution for the Egyptians. It punishes evil, but is capable of becoming an embodiment of evil. It is to serve Moshe as a sign to the Jewish people proving Hashem's appearance to him to assure him that they will believe him, but simultaneously chastises him for having stated that they would not believe! In the hand it is a manifestation of the Divine, stretching back to the Creation; cast to the earth it is a manifestation of that primal evil which also originates at the beginning of time.

Let us go yet deeper. There is an idea that evil is not created in the world; however it is certainly made *possible*. Changing that possibility into a *reality* is our choice. If we do not pervert the world, it remains good. If we deflect it from its natural state *we* bring evil into being. There is a mystical source which indicates that the higher worlds are created straight and that this finite, physical world represents a "bending" of that straightness. Once a "bend" has occurred, there is a danger. When all is straight, no error can be made. When a bend manifests, error has not become inevitable but it has become decidedly possible.

A *mashal* (allegory) will make this clear. If a person walks along a perfectly straight road he can *never* lose sight of his point of origin — all that is required is to turn around and look back and it will be clearly seen. But once the road forks, once the traveller has turned onto a road which is at an angle to his previous path, he can no longer see home. When he looks back he sees only a lonely fork in a lonely road. It becomes possible to forget where the origin is. And that is how the world is built. The higher worlds are straight and the angelic inhabitants of those worlds see reality plainly, undeniably, and of course are not free to forget it. But we, inhabitants of the finite, see only the finite as a point of origin. To see the spiritual one must be able to *see around corners!* One has to be able to see into a dimension which is essentially invisible from here. *The very fact of a finite Creation intrinsically hides the spiritual.* Of course that is not bad — it provides the framework within which to exercise free will; one can look at the world and *choose* to see its incredible beauty, its plan-and-purpose, its glow. That is the correct utilization of the smokescreen of the world — to penetrate it. But one can just as easily see it as skin-deep, finite only, filled with random accident, and *that* is bad. Good and bad lie only in the choice of perception.

The effort of seeing the invisible, of seeing around corners, is called "remembering". The Torah *mitzva* of remembering — deeply, spiritually — is the *mitzva* of opening a pathway to higher perception. *Remembering* the Creation, our origin as a people at the exodus from Egypt, our origin as the people of the Torah at Sinai, is our lifeline. In fact the command to remember Sinai is phrased thus "Be careful and guard your soul well *lest you forget* the things which your eyes have seen .... the day on which you stood before Hashem at Chorev (Sinai)". Not "remember", but "lest you forget" — the *natural condition* of the Jewish people is remembrance. We are *always* at Sinai, that is our natural mode, we need only take care not to forget it!

"Atem eidai — You are my witnesses"; Hashem appoints us His witnesses from Sinai on. Witnesses are called in only when

the original subject of their testimony is no longer visible. Their task is to *recall* the events.

To straighten what is bent. That is our task. Not to be deceived by a bend in the road. The name of the Jewish people ישראל (Israel) spells ישר אל the *straight one* of Hashem! And the other classical name by which we are called is ישרון (Yeshurun) which spells ישר *straight* to the "ן" the letter which indicates the fiftieth level, the level of transcendence. In fact, the word which tells the story of the entire Creation בראשית ("In the beginning") can be arranged to spell ישר אבת *straight* from "א" to "ב" (the beginning of all creation, all movement), or straight from the "אב" the Father, the point of origin itself, to "ת", the final letter, the letter of completion.

Unwavering straightness. When Hashem created man, says the *midrash*, He showed him around the Garden. "See how beautiful is My world, take care that you do not destroy it." *My* world is beautiful: *you* have the power to destroy it. "And Hashem made man *straight*, but they (humans) complicated things." Adam chose to eat the fruit and the potential for evil became real.

*　　*　　*

Now let us return to the *mateh*. The mystical source we referred to earlier explains that the word *mateh*, a staff, is from the root meaning *to bend* נטה, or to *tend* in a particular direction, or to stretch out from the source (*Noteh shamayim ve'yosed aretz* — He extends the Heavens and founds the earth). In fact, a staff is really a *branch*, that which branches, bends, away from the trunk. That is why the word *mateh* in Hebrew means a staff and *also* a tribe — the twelve tribes are each a *branch* of their father Yaakov; his centrality and oneness splits into twelve different directions in his sons. This observation is no accident: the other Hebrew word for a staff is שבט (shevet) and *this word too* means a tribe!

So the *mateh*, somehow, stands at the junction between heaven and earth. It is located at the point where the straight bends. It is in fact an agent of Creation, poised to reveal the straight bright line of Hashem's presence in the world — it is the immediate agent of miracles; when it appears, the world obeys. But it is ever ready to manifest as the reflection of all evil. Its natural place is in the human hand, the hand of Adam at the time of Creation, the hand of Avraham, Yitzchak, Yaakov, Yosef, Moshe Rabbeinu. In these hands it is pure sapphire-clear mastery of the world. But cast to the earth, or in deeper terms: brought low, close to dark physicality, it becomes pure terror. And its correction? Pick it up by the tail; treat it *as if it were a mateh;* relate to it while yet dumb with terror as it should have been held all along, then, and only then, *after* it has been thus conquered does it reveal its true identity, its sanctity. It is in reality a *mateh,* and yet the serpent was no illusion.

$$* \quad * \quad *$$

That is the secret of the *mateh,* and that is its mysterious duality. Let us now apply this understanding to the events we struggled to fathom earlier. At the burning bush, while facing the ultimate Reality directly, Moshe Rabbeinu is taught the lesson of the *mateh.* Armed with the tool he needs, the consummate control of reality when it is grasped in *kedusha* (holiness), he enters Egypt, the domain of evil. The Jewish people are enslaved in Egypt; in deeper terms they are oppressed by the forces of evil. That is why they are there, to become a people that is holy by breaking out of the dimension of impurity. And their leader, Moshe, must face the king of evil, Pharaoh, in the ultimate showdown. This is no cheap magic contest, no attempt to prove whose sorcery is stronger — that is not Torah. It is a dialogue between good and evil at the highest level; good must conquer evil at that level, at the formation of the Jewish people; and it is enshrined in a *parsha* (portion) in Torah.

Pharaoh denies knowledge of Hashem. Of course. Moshe demonstrates: Pharaoh, what you are doing is misrepresenting reality, you are transforming the *mateh* of the world into the primal *nachash* (serpent)! And Pharaoh's response? *That is our business!* That is what Egypt is, that is what we teach here! His wife does the same. The children do the same. All of Egypt is intrinsically dedicated to perverting the spiritual truth into unholiness. You are bringing produce to an overstocked market! No simple witty remark, but a deep statement of Egypt's manifesto. And Moshe's reply? Of course I must bring my produce here; here is where the experts should recognize quality! Here is the very place, the only place, to distinguish between the tricky, shimmering facets of perception of good and evil. And Aharon's staff swallows up all the others — good and holiness will engulf evil eventually. And *of course* it swallows them after revealing itself as a *mateh*, not a serpent; *that is the point:* it is the reality of correct perception, of remaining true to the source of the world that will conquer the vicious falsehood of evil.

The business of evil is to dash the *mateh* to earth and cause it to manifest as the *nachash*. Our business is to hold it aloft and reveal it as the *mateh*. It is not easy. Once the road has forked one may be genuinely lost. Fighting home may take all we have. But that moment of transformation *of the self,* that point of snapping out of a terrifying ordeal into the transcendent clarity of victory is what life is about. And that is why we are here.

Chapter 7

Beyond Astrology

Wwe have studied some facets of the idea that our work must be to break the limitations of the natural, to live on a plane above the natural. To understand just how far this obligation extends, we need to study an area which itself is above the physical earthly plane and yet which presents a danger, an obstruction to spiritual growth. This area comprises the related subjects of astrology and idolatry.

Astrology and idolatry have certain elements in common. Let us study some of their common ground in order to understand more clearly our role as a transcendent people, both individually and nationally.

The Torah's prohibition of idolatry (*avoda zara*) prompts some particularly puzzling questions. Firstly, when the Torah prohibits us from serving "other gods", exactly which "other gods" are being referred to? The common conception of idolatrous gods is that they are imaginary, figments of a fertile imagination. Worship of graven images is exactly that: people bowing to statues, pictures or other physical objects. But if these "gods" are no more than lifeless statues or simply dreamed-up ideas, why does the Torah relate to them as if they are real? Many verses refer to gods other than Hashem as if they are very real indeed: *"Mi chamocha ba'eilim Hashem* — Who is like You among the *gods*, Hashem?"* (To translate *eilim* as "mighty ones" meaning human leaders is obviously wrong — what comparison could there possibly be between them and Hashem?) *"Ki kol elohei ha'amim elilim* — For all the *gods* of the nations are small gods"; *"Ki Keil gadol Hashem umelech gadol al kol elohim* — For Hashem is a great G-d and a great King over all *gods"*. Who are these *elohim acheirim,* "other gods"?

Secondly, we note that the Torah's greatest prohibition is idolatry; it is the first of all the negative commandments and mystically contains all of them. Surely if idolatry were no more than a ridiculous misconception the Torah would not prohibit it thus. It would be enough to say "Do not be gullible", or even "Do not be fools"! The root prohibition of the Torah must surely be posed against something of very real existence and danger. Again, we are forced to conclude that in the sources of idolatry lurks something all too real.

Thirdly, from a deeper perspective, we note that the Torah uses names for these "other gods" which are some of the very names which are Hashem's! *Elohim acheirim* other gods; *eilim* gods — these names are profane versions of Hashem's names; said without holiness, to be sure, but the same names nevertheless. Although we never find Hashem's "name of essence" used thus, we certainly see His other names so used. All this implies that we must take the issue of idolatry much more seriously than simply dismissing it as primitive nonsense irrelevant to people of maturity.

*   *   *

The answer lies in understanding some of the deeper levels which form the foundation of the Creation. The Nefesh Hachaim and many other sources tell us that there are many interlocking levels to the Creation. In an infinitely stretching chain beginning at the very Source of existence, many worlds are connected in sequence. Each of these higher worlds infuses the level below it with existence and energy; each is "male" with regard to the world below it which is, relatively speaking, "female", and together they "bring out" yet another level below them. This process continues in myriad complexity until finally our finite world results.

Each level has its own uniqueness, but let us focus on one in particular for our present purpose. Between all the higher worlds and our concrete physical one, there is a stage which is intermediate. This stage, or world, is not directly perceived by us, but *is accessible*. Its function is to transmit the higher energies down to this world — both the creative energy that forms the various aspects of this level and the directing *hashgacha* or Divine guidance which manipulates the affairs of our world. It is, if you like, the interface between all the higher worlds and ours. It is the limit of that which can be perceived from our perspective. This intermediate level is the world of the stars, the zodiac, known as the *mazalos*.

In fact, the word *mazal*, commonly translated as "luck", really means a "flow" (נזל), as in the flow of a liquid, because it represents the "flow" of energy from a higher level down to this one. Of course there could not be a more inaccurate translation than "luck"! The concept of "luck" implies total randomness, "*mazal*" is just the opposite; only the source of the directing

Hand behind it is *hidden*, which is why it is so easily perceived by us as random.

Astrology is the science of understanding this intermediate world and using the knowledge of its structure and changes to predict events in the physical world. Strictly speaking it is not reading the future at all, *that* is prophesy; it is simply reading the *present*. One who knows the stars can tell what will happen here because the causative energies are disposed that way *now*, the forces are already in action. A simple analogy would be: if one showed a seed to an expert, he could predict what tree would grow from that seed many years hence even though the non-expert would see no more than an undifferentiated seed; the expert is not seeing the future, he simply knows seeds! And particular seeds become particular trees naturally and predictably. That is exactly the point about astrology — it is not a transcendent wisdom, it is a knowledge of the root of the natural.

*   *   *

Let us go further and apply this to idolatry. The root dimension of the *mazalos* "splits" the higher energy into various "channels", each channel being the root of certain energies within nature, and these defined and specific energies manifest as the details of the natural world and its events. Idolatry, in essence, is the idea of relating not to the supernal Source of all existence, the ultimate Oneness, but to the *channels which bring down energy* into the world, the "openings of the pipelines". An idolater focuses on the zodiac (*avodas kochavim u'mazalos* — the worship of stars and zodiac) or on various forces of nature: the sun, the wind, the rain. His graven images are tangible representations of these deeper energies (an idolater who literally worships his piece of wood or stone as divine has transgressed the prohibition of being foolish long before the prohibition of idolatry!) Of course one who serves the ineffable Source could never create a physical representation; one whose perception goes no further than a source of the natural can.

The Rambam says that originally, close to the beginning of the world's history people acknowledged Hashem. Then came a stage when people reasoned as follows: since Hashem uses agencies such as the forces of nature to accomplish His will, surely it would be fitting to give honor to these forces as His emissaries, His viceroys? They began to accord honor to the intermediates as well as to Hashem. And eventually, they forgot about Hashem! Such was the development of the idea of idolatry. What needs further study, though, is: what was the underlying motivation in this error? Such slips are not casual. In fact, the underlying reason for forgetting the Source and remembering the intermediate levels is the most basic of all vested interests: selfishness. Let us understand.

The real difference between worship of the Source and worship of intermediaries is as follows. One who serves the Source is concerned about what his obligations are; what does Hashem demand of me? How do I sacrifice myself, give myself to Hashem? One who serves the intermediaries is concerned about *what they can do for him:* the intermediaries are, after all, the immediate source of all human needs, all natural functions of the world. The idolater looks to the immediate source of power, love, wealth — in fact of all his needs and asks: How can they serve me? He does not need to go further, to relate to the absolute source. Rabbi Simcha Wasserman זצ"ל used to say that idolatry is like the behavior of an individual who enters a department store and wants an object which is too expensive for his liking. He offers the clerk behind the counter a bribe so that he should hand him the object. He is prepared to pay the price of the bribe, but not the full price of the object. He relates to the departmental clerk but does not concern himself with the owner of the store — the owner does not deliver the goods, the clerk does. So too an idolater: he is prepared to pay some price for his needs but not the full price; the full price required for genuine service is *all you have*, and that is too much for him. He seeks to pay off the source which *delivers the goods*, that is his concern, but Hashem, the overall owner of the whole enterprise, is not his concern at all. *Where can I obtain the goods?* One has only to consider the gods of ancient Greece: a god of love, a god of war, a god of fertility — but no one god who created the world! That is irrelevant when you seek only "the goods".

Correctly understood, the heart of the difference is this: true service understands that Hashem is everything, I am only to serve; idolatry understands that *I am everything,* and *my gods are to serve me!* It states: *tzaddikim* (righteous individuals), their G-d stands over them, as it says "And Hashem was standing over him" (at Yaakov's dream of the ladder) whereas *resha'im* (evil individuals) *stand over their gods,* as it says "And Pharaoh was standing over the river" (the Nile was the Egyptian deity). Diametric opposites: who counts, and where is reality? If Hashem counts and He is the source of reality — that is worship. But if I count and reality is the world of my personal desires, that is idolatry.

This also explains why images of idolatrous worship are often human in form — idolatry is really worship of the self and the graven images are projections of the self. Astrology — intermediates, and idolatry — their worship.

*   *   *

We can now answer the questions with which we began. "Other gods" are not imaginary at all; they are the genuine and Divinely created transmitters of Hashem's energy to the world. Their names are His because they are the agents of His manifestation here. What is false about them is the mistake of considering them to have independent power, of being free to accept bribes, of being sources in their own right. There is a hand which gives: idolatry focuses on the hand only and ignores the One behind the hand; true spirituality seeks to cleave to the Giver.

*   *   *

We find Avraham Avinu arguing with Hashem — he is told prophetically that he will have a son, yet he argues: How can that be, he asks Hashem, since the stars predict otherwise? How do we understand a man arguing with Hashem Himself on the strength of astrological prediction? Surely Hashem's explicit word overrides astrology? The answer is that the stars too, are Hashem's words. He writes the book of the heavens. Therefore Avraham asks: But Hashem, Your word to me is contradicted by Your word in the stars! Hashem answers by teaching him the great secret of Jewish existence, "And he took him outside"; simply, outside his tent, but mystically, *outside the sphere of the stars!* You are not bound by those channels, Hashem teaches him. They are natural, they define the inevitable; you are transcendent, you can define your own destiny. Of course, we must remember that Avraham merited to be carried above the world and the zodiac because he behaved in a superhuman way: he withstood trials in a fashion which generated transcendence. The message is: if you live on the higher plane, it becomes real.

The *gemara* tells of many incidents illustrating this, and how even one *mitzva* can change a destiny. A young girl was destined to die on her wedding day, according to expert astrological prediction. On that day, during the wedding meal, she took a hairpin from her hair and unconsciously inserted it into the wall near her — and transfixed a cobra which was poised to strike her! When she was asked what her merit was it emerged that in the midst of her wedding celebration, at that happiest moment, she had taken food out to a beggar who had remained unnoticed by all the guests. A *mitzva* is performed, a physical act which originates and generates transcendence, and a person's destiny is altered.

Mitzvos live on the higher plane. The root of the word *"mitzva"* is closely related to צוותא "togetherness", because a *mitzva* brings us together with Hashem. An act which has the potential to lift the one who performs it into direct relationship with the Source of all existence certainly has a power far greater than mere intermediate levels.

The Sfas Emes says that when Hashem wills an action and we carry it out, we become one with Him. His *ratzon* (desire) at the Supernal level formulates a command; that command, a direct expression of His will, is brought down and formulated as a commandment of the Torah. We then *make His will our will*, we desire to carry out that commandment, and we carry it out in the finite, physical world. His will is done. Together, we have closed a cosmic circuit: the circuit begins at the highest level possible and we bring it into action. The voltage is indescribable, the flow of current infinite. *Together* we have become one cycle of cause and effect. And as we form the desire in our minds to do His will, we become a miniature version of the entire process — a true *tzelem Elokim* (image of Hashem)! Together in the sense of our reflecting Him, as it were, and together in the sense of a partnership with one purpose carried out by the harmony of desire of the partners.

It follows then, that when we do other than the will of Hashem we are tearing ourselves away from reality. The time spent in such activity is time out of the circuit of existence, time wasted in purely physical levels with no higher energy being drawn into them.

And just as a *mitzva* correctly performed has the power to bond us with the Source, to make us part of the cause of existence instead of merely part of the effects, conversely, and frighteningly, the *gemara* states that the consequence of attaching importance to astrology, of seeking divination and astrological prediction, is that *the predicted event becomes inevitable!* One who insists on living only within the natural becomes subject to it. One may discover information about a forthcoming event, but in so doing one may become its victim. The *gemara Yerushalmi*, in explaining the verse *"ki lo nachash b'Yaakov* — For there is no divination in Yaakov"* states that the word *"lo"* can be read in two ways: "there is not" or "there is to him"; there is no divining in the Jewish people, but if one gives credence to such things, if one seeks divination "it *is* to him" — it becomes active.

The entire purpose of the Jewish people is to live above nature. Our challenge is to rise to the dimension of Hashem's will, the dimension where limits are set only by our own inertia, and not to live in the mechanical. Our test and our challenge is to enter the source dimension. Failure is to be locked into the natural, the inevitable. Success is to break through to the source.

II.

Structure
of the
Mind

Chapter 8

Silence

I. KNOWLEDGE

Just as time and human experience have phases of limitation and transcendence, so too does the mind. Perhaps the best way to express this idea is to say that just as the human comprises body and *neshama* (soul), the mind itself comprises an outer, more earthbound layer, and an inner more elevated core. The problem is that there are no words to describe the inner mind, yet we are forced to seek it because it is that which makes us human, Jewish and the unique individual each of us is. Let us grapple with this problem and despite the difficulty of communication, attempt to clarify this most important subject.

The inner mind is the vessel of knowledge — *da'as*. The *gemara* states "*D'da bei, kula bei; d'lo da bei, ma bei?* — He who has it has everything; he who does not have it, what does he have?" There are even sharper statements than this about one who has no *da'as,* inner knowledge. The *gemara* expresses the problem of lack of *da'as* thus: *"Mi she'ein bo de'a, assur l'rachem alav"* — one cannot show certain kinds of *rachmanus,* beneficence, to one who has no *da'as*-wisdom. This is understood as meaning that just as one may not give money to a drug addict — that would only worsen his situation, so too one is forced to withhold certain benefits from a person who has so little *da'as* that he will only damage himself with what is provided for him.

The faculty of *da'as* considers, weighs up, makes decisions. It is capable of deciding correctly even when the sides of the question at hand are evenly weighted: *da'as Torah* is that unique, priceless ability of a person great in Torah to define the correct course of action even when the options seem balanced; it is that deep and sensitive.

In fact, all value is concentrated here: the Torah unit of currency is the *shekel* — the root of this unit of value means to weigh up, to compare (לשקול). And therefore all *kinyan,* all acquisition, is a function of *da'as.* A child has no *da'as,* and a child's dealings are contractually invalid. At *bar-mitzva* age the *da'as* "comes in", and from then a young person's actions are contractually valid; he or she can activate *kinyanim,* acquisitions, legally. Says the *gemara "Da kani, ma chaser? Da lo kani, ma kani? —* If you have acquired it *(da'as),* what do you lack? And if you lack it, what have you acquired?"* No *kinyan* is possible without *da'as.* No acquisition; and in the broader sense, no growth.

And hence the desperately pathetic situation of one who has no *da'as* — unable even to receive. It has been said in bitter humor that one who lacks *da'as* so thoroughly that he cannot even receive *rachmanus* is *really* in need of *rachmanus!*

What is the nature of this special knowledge?

Many words and much explanation are needed to convey

this idea. When it is grasped, it is so fundamental, so primary, so obvious, that one wonders why so many words were necessary. It is like one who teaches a skill: no amount of words is enough to convey the nuances of style which add up to that skill. But the instructor talks and demonstrates in order that the student gets close enough to the desired goal so that he eventually gets the idea almost accidentally; when he has it, it is obvious and is never lost. Of course, it will take him great effort to teach it to another student. In fact, the very definition of the *da'as* is that words are irrelevant to it, words cannot exist in it. And yet, one must remember that all deeper wisdom is simply a description of reality: if one is sensitive, it will be recognized.

*　　*　　*

Perhaps the best way to approach the subject of *da'as* is by exclusion — to understand which parts of the mind are not included in it. By drawing a contrast between the categories of the mind, the *da'as* may be entered. The classic formulation of this idea is Rabbi Dessler's, and he explains as follows.

There are two parts to the mind — an outer part, the *mabat ha'chitzoni*, the "outer view" or "outer eye", and the inner part, the *mabat ha'pnimi*, the "inner view" or "inner eye". The "outer eye" is easy to define in words: it is that part of the mind which grasps the world through the five senses, and it includes the rational or logical faculty. It deals therefore with the finite, the measurable, the arithmetical, the logical. Anything which this faculty can grasp can be expressed in words, can be tested and proved. Perfect communication can be achieved between people at this level. Everything in the physical world is essentially accessible to this form of knowledge; and perhaps most significantly, a machine can duplicate its functions (often more efficiently than the human — computers and calculators, for example).

All the aspects of our consciousness, and consciousness itself, which are not included in this definition, comprise the "inner eye", the *da'as*. The *da'as* is intrinsic knowledge. It grasps things *as they are* and *because they are*, not because they can be measured or proved or expressed. In fact, the things which the *da'as* knows can *never* be expressed, proved or measured. They are never physical or finite. No machine could ever contain any of the knowledge of the *da'as*. This inner aspect of knowledge is *you*, the real you. The outer mechanical aspects of the mind which can be duplicated by machine are not you, they are simply your tools, attributes which the inner mind uses to communicate with the world. Things which you know externally are simply registered like elements in a computer program; things which you know internally are not registered, they are the inner knowledge itself.

"*Da'as*" actually means intimate communion. Intimate marriage is referred to as "knowledge" by the Torah, *da'as*. This is because the inner mind and its knowledge are truly, inextricably bound into one. The mystics say that if you know something with the external mind and it proves to be false, it is simply deleted from the mind; but if something grasped by the inner mind ever proved to be false, *you would cease to exist*. It is the essence of intimacy. Of course, nothing grasped by the *da'as* could ever be false, it is the vessel of truth. In the pure heart of *da'as* one understands or fails to understand, but never understands wrongly.

* * *

What are the elements which the *da'as* holds? A brief consideration shows that they are all the things which are most important in one's inner life. Some of the components of *da'as* are: the knowledge of one's own existence (this is the primary knowledge of the *da'as*); the knowledge of the present; the knowledge of one's own free will; the grasp that life has meaning; the grasp of intrinsic right and wrong; and ultimately, the *da'as* is the vessel of consciousness of a transcendent reality (the mystics say that this is really an expansion of the most primary knowledge of the *da'as*, that I exist — one of Hashem's names is "*Ani*", the infinite "I").

An examination of this list will show that although these issues are certainly critically important to the concept of being human, they cannot be proved. Although one knows them most profoundly, they cannot be put into words. No matter how much one professes the reality of morality, an obstinate skeptic is free to deny it. No-one has yet formally proved that "I exist" — this is the oldest problem in philosophy. ("I think, therefore I am" does *not* mean that my existence is proved because my brain functions physiologically — that is no more proof than the physiology of any other bodily organ; it is simply a basic statement of the *da'as*: "*I know I am*, therefore I am" is really what it means. Of course, since there are no words for the issues of the *da'as*, it must simply be stated as "I think, therefore...." and an initiate will understand.)

* * *

The dilemma is obvious. How are all these areas to be

examined, refined, elevated in the mind if they cannot be proved or expressed? How can one ever begin to think about them logically? The answer is simple and staggering. Just as the external mind must be used to grasp those things which are accessible to it, so too the *da'as* itself must be used for its material. One must never attempt to use the one mode for the material of the other. In a most striking illustration of this, Rabbi Dessler explains that the external mind is like a camera. A camera can take a picture of anything in the world, *except the camera itself!* The camera cannot be turned in on itself without breaking. The outer mind's logical, arithmetical finite eye can never be focused on the inner zone. It must always be focused outward, at the external world, and the raw, intrinsic wholesome faculty of *da'as* must be used to grasp its own existence and facets.

I know I exist *intrinsically*, axiomatically. I do *not need* any particular sensory input to be aware that I exist. I simply know it, most profoundly and powerfully. One who cannot feel, taste, hear, see or smell is most certainly not without consciousness of his own existence. All the contents of the *da'as* are known thus, they are first principles. If proof is attempted, it collapses.

*   *   *

There are certain exercises which can be used to grasp the sharp distinction between these two dimensions, the inner and the outer. One of these is common to many young people — most adolescents have had the experience of looking up at the sky and wondering: where does it end? A common result of this question is the following private, inner dialogue: "It does not end, it goes on forever." A few seconds later: "But that's impossible. There must be an end *somewhere*. Of course there is an end." And a few seconds later: "But what's beyond that end? There must be *something* beyond. Of course there is, it goes on forever." And so on! This is simply an example of the rapid oscillation between using the inner and outer modes alternately — the *da'as* is comfortable with infinity, but the outer wisdom *cannot handle* that idea; it immediately challenges the *da'as* by trying to analyze it. Of course it cannot, the camera breaks, and the *da'as* is free. Until the "camera" recovers and tries again. Is this oscillation not a common experience when one attempts to think about the Divine?

A classic experience which frees the *da'as* is abject terror. If a person is travelling, say by aircraft, philosophically pondering whether or not he exists, and the aircraft suddenly begins to shake violently, it is impossible at that moment to dismiss the notion of one's existence. In fact, the *only* consciousness at that moment is "Don't let me die!" (or "My child!" which is an extension of the same emotion). Fear suitably paralyzes the outer faculty and a rich experience of one's existence remains.

Equally powerful is the ecstasy of being alive which is felt for a few moments after one was in mortal danger. A sage once described the experience of being drawn under the waves in the ocean until he almost lost consciousness. At that moment, he broke the surface and gasped a life-saving breath of air. "That was a breath of pure *da'as*", is the way he described the superconsciousness of being alive when that simple fact was critically held in the balance.

(The mystics explain that the root of all pleasure is really a heightened sense of being alive; that is why when we make a blessing on the *pleasure* of food (*birkas ha'nehenin*) the wording is "Blessed is He who *gives life* to the worlds"! We use the experience of pleasure to bring to conscious awareness the fact of being alive — we take the opportunity to make a blessing on life itself.)

* * *

A direct building of the *da'as* is true meditation. Here too, the words are necessarily misleading. Those who understand meditation teach that one must "switch off the mind" in order to meditate. This instruction, like all *da'as* experiences clumsily put into words, is exactly the opposite of what an initiate understands. "Switching off" the mind is not meditation, it is unconsciousness! Relaxing perhaps, but not meditation. Meditation is a "switching *on*" of the mind! But of course these words are meaningless, so the instruction is to switch off; however, what is meant is to switch off the *external mind,* that is *exactly* the way to activate the *da'as.* Since the two are by definition in conflict, the *da'as* seeking to transcend and the outer wisdom seeking to hold in the finite, the battle must be stopped before inner knowledge can flourish. All this is actually obvious, it must simply be recognized.

* * *

In fact, the relationship between inner and outer wisdom is much deeper. Although their modes are in conflict, they are bonded to each other. (The idea of intimate bonding inherent in *da'as* should be apparent here.) Some thought will show that even the external facts which the mind registers are not simply registered in machine-like fashion; once they are registered they are also *grasped, understood,* as part of consciousness. In other words, there are external facts which are logical, amenable to proof and expressible in finite terms which enter the external mind, but thereafter they *bond* with the mind, the *da'as* acts on them, takes them in, *knows* them intimately.

The *da'as* makes the difference between registering a fact and understanding it. A classic experience which illustrates this is that of grappling with a problem for hours and not seeing the solution, or sometimes even having the solution but not understanding it, not connecting with it. Typically, one gives up in exhaustion and goes to sleep. Very often, one wakes the next morning with "I've got it! I understand!" There are mystical sources which explain that this happens because powerful logical thought may *shrink* the *da'as* while it occupies the mind; however, sleep *stills* the driving of the logical, the limited, and *da'as* takes over; it is *because* one stopped thinking about the problem that one understood it! Words are inadequate here; one who has experienced this will need no words.

Being human requires both faculties: external information gleaned from interaction with the world and analyzed clearly by the calculator or computer function of the brain, and the inner grasp of that information which no machine could ever do. Information without grasp, without understanding, is not human. Understanding without information is impossible — bonding must occur *to something.* This is the meaning of the *mishna:* "*Im ein da'as, ein bina; im ein bina, ein da'as —* If there is no *da'as* there is no *bina* (logical, analytical knowledge); if there is no *bina* there is no *da'as.*" Of course this formulation means that one cannot have even the *least amount* of either without the other: they must always be acquired simultaneously.

*   *   *

It is the bonding of inner and outer wisdom and their harmony which is the beauty of the mind; that inner marriage which is the core of our being. When the two bond correctly, the outer wisdom remaining under control, subjecting its input to the grasp of the *da'as,* and the *da'as* understanding all of the outer wisdom appropriately, then thought is fruitful. Only when the male and female elements of thought blend can fertile, creative thought-energy be generated. This is the secret of the *bar-mitzva:* the child acquires *da'as* when his *body* becomes fertile.

To use the terms of our pattern: the outer mind is the lower, the finite, bounded by the natural. The inner mind, the *da'as,* is the higher, essentially human, essentially unlimited. The lower faculty is relatively easy to train and develop, the higher faculty a lifetime's challenge. That is exactly our challenge; to rise above the purely finite, the mechanical, and to open wide the faculty of *da'as,* to begin with the simple and profound awareness of "I am" and to strive towards sensing the higher Existence, towards *knowing* that Existence essentially, intrinsically. That is the purpose of *da'as,* the vessel of real knowledge.

*   *   *

The final redemption, the revelation, will be a revelation of *da'as.* Knowledge of the higher Reality, of Hashem Himself, is the purpose of existence. The Rambam states that the purpose of the world's creation was to form an *"uma she'hi yoda'as es Hashem"* — a nation which knows Hashem"; "knows" with the wisdom of *da'as.* "Ki mal'a ha'aretz de'a* — For the earth shall be filled with knowledge", the real knowledge. *"Haskel v'yado'a osi* — Become wise and *know* Me".

We must open that vessel of the *neshama* which can be filled with such knowledge. A sage of this generation has said that we dare not allow ourselves to be so deficient in *da'as* that we cannot merit the *rachmanus* we so desperately need. If we open the vessel, it will be filled.

II. SILENCE

The tool most needed to develop inner knowledge is silence. Since all of the inner wisdom can never be put into words, only silence can contain it. Let us strive to understand.

Words are finite. Words, no matter how perfectly chosen and eloquent, are fragments of meaning. They are the bits and pieces which communication struggles to construct. One who is sensitive knows that the deeper the experience and the closer to one's core the subject being communicated, the more difficult it is to express. The most significant things to be shared in life require no words, demand silence. Words intrude at these times, reduce the moment to a parody of its real self. There is a particular agony in most powerfully needing to share the most beautiful moments, experiences, and being unable to put them into words. The cure for that pain is to share with one who has his or her own inner awareness of such things; then words are entirely unnecessary.

There is an idea that words must lie. They can never accurately reconstruct consciousness. The Hebrew alphabet begins אבגד. The first letter א (aleph) indicates mystical knowledge, higher wisdom — its numerical value is one, a clue to the Supernal Oneness. Its components are a higher *yud* and a lower, mirrored *yud*, joined by a *vav*, the letter of connection, which together comprise twenty-six, the numerical value of Hashem's name. There are many more secrets hidden in the *aleph*, but the one to note here is that *it is silent*. All-encompassing higher knowledge has no finite sound. The next three letters, the coming down into the finite, the tangible, are בגד in sequence spelling *beged*, the word for a garment, the outer clothing of the invisible core. But amazingly, wonderfully, בגד a "garment", is also the word for "treachery". The garments may lie, they may cover an identity instead of reveal it, that is their nature. The silent center cannot lie, but its outer layers, those layers which have sound, which speak, may speak treachery. (The Hebrew word for an outer garment, a coat מעיל is similar; the same root spells מעילה a profaning of the holy, a betrayal of holiness.)

*　*　*

That is the problem with words. The Maharal explains that Moshe Rabbeinu (Moses) could not speak well because of this idea. The conventional understanding is that he suffered from a speech defect, an imperfection. But the opposite is true: he could not speak well because of his perfection! He was holding in a world of truth, where things are grasped as they are, grasped by a pure *da'as*. Things grasped thus prophetically, essentially, could never be shrunk into words! To do so would be to reduce Divine knowledge to a finite level. Then, after the *miracle* of the giving of the Torah at Sinai *which was exactly that:* a condensing of the Divine word somehow, miraculously, into the words of Torah, Moshe spoke normally! (As it says: *"Eleh ha'dvarim asher diber Moshe* — These are the words which *Moshe spoke.")* It takes a miracle for higher truth to be spoken here, to "clothe" essence appropriately and not to "betray" it.

This is the secret behind the hiddenness of mystical teachings. The name for such teaching is *sod*, "secret". The uninitiated understand that the word "secret" is used because this wisdom is *kept secret*, no-one will tell you. But this is not so; the word "secret" is used because this wisdom *cannot* be told, it can never be put into words! Even when one *knows* the "secret", it remains secret!

A most potent illustration of the constricting effect of speech is found in the *aggadic* description of the process of birth. The fetus learns Torah with an angel, as we have noted previously. When the unborn child knows all of the Torah in the deepest way and begins the process of transition into this world, the angel strikes him on the mouth and he forgets all that he knew. This is strange: why a blow on the mouth? Surely a blow on the head is more appropriate to causing forgetfulness? But the inexpressibly beautiful idea being taught here, say the mystical sources, is that the blow on the mouth is the *gift of speech!* A blow, mystically, is always a challenge to grow, to develop a new faculty or level, and *on the mouth* because that is the organ of speech. As the child gains the nucleus of the ability to formulate finite words, he loses the clear, intimate knowledge of the higher wisdom! Not just simultaneously, but *because* of the gift of speech — being articulate means being able to shrink things into definite, bounded form; and that is exactly the opposite of being able to expand things into their unlimited essence. And only miracle can reconnect the two — miracle, or the work of intense silence.

Silence develops the deep well of the personality. This is an obligation, not a luxury. There must always be more to the personality than that which can be expressed. If you can sum up what you are in a few minutes of talking, you are just that — a few sentences from beginning to end. No matter how much is discovered, revealed, there must be infinitely more. There is a most moving and deep Torah illustration of this idea. When David Hamelech brought the Holy Ark up to Jerusalem he danced in front of it in joy and ecstasy. The verses describe his dancing in the most expressive way; David was demonstrating his honor of Hashem by dancing thus in public.

When he approaches his home, his wife Michal, daughter of Saul, objects and chastises him for conducting himself in such unbecoming fashion in public. She accuses him of having been immodestly exposed in the eyes of the maidservants and the people *"k'echad ha'reikim* — like one of the empty fellows"*. David responds sharply by explaining that for Hashem's honor his own is not to be considered; he tells her that he would like to do even more: in the eyes of those same maidservants *"un'kalosi od mi'zos* — I will be even lighter than this"*, he says. The next verses indicate that because of her improper criticism, Michal had no child until the day of her death, and a close reading of the text indicates that in fact she had a child on the last day of her life, she died in childbirth.

What is the meaning of this exchange? What exactly was Michal's concern? What was David's reply? What is the connection with such childbirth and why is the consequence so serious? Was she concerned because he revealed himself bodily, physically — perhaps his ankles? All Torah has unlimited depth; what is below the surface here?

There is an insight into this narrative which is exquisite in its revealing of our subject. David was not revealing his ankles; that was not the problem. He was revealing his *neshama*, his soul. Dance is a very powerful expression of internality; there is an idea that one can tell if a man has depth from the way he walks, all the more so from dance. David's dancing showed such power that Michal felt he had exposed his entire *neshama* in those Jerusalem streets (*k'echad ha'reikim* — like one of the *empty* fellows!) and that is never allowed! There is a deep obligation to retain far more depth than that which one reveals. If all has been revealed, made explicit, where is the connection to the source, to the deep well of spirituality?

We can only imagine the intensity of the scene — Michal was a very great woman and she felt she had seen to the very depth of David's *neshama*; his dance must have been an expression of pure spiritual fire. And David's reply unforgettable: "I shall go further than this" — in other words: "Do you think that what you saw revealed is *all there is?* There is *far more* unrevealed than what you perceived! I have not forgotten that very same obligation of nurturing and building depth which concerns you. But you have misjudged my depth." That is how surely it was hidden!

And it could be that Michal's misperception of her great husband, indescribably great though she herself was and perhaps because of it, was somehow connected to her bringing forth a child with her life — that ultimate act of bringing the hidden into the revealed.

Chapter 9

Desire

I. DESIRE

Just as the body has its root in the *neshama* (soul), so too the inner wisdom has a higher root. This root of wisdom is *ratzon*, desire. In this source lies the origin of all inner life. The outer mind can never initiate, it can only respond. The inner mind is all initiative, and its own beginning is desire.

Every process has a beginning. Before the process begins there is nothing, emptiness. Suddenly, there is something — the flash of an idea, the surge of energy which the mind feels at the beginning of a project. At the interface between that emptiness, that potential, and the very first spark of thought, is desire. It is the motivating energy of bringing something into being from nothing. Of course, it is infinitely short-lived: once we become aware of the thought it is present, already formed. But the moment of flashing-in leaves a residue of energy in the mind, a "high", and we can savor it briefly.

Before anything can happen it must be motivated, and that motivation is *ratzon* — "desire" or "will". It is the flash of conception.

This *ratzon* is a mysterious force in the mind. It is the source of all inner life. The numerical value of רצון *ratzon* is also that of מקור "source"; and of שמו "His Name" — the ultimate source. No thought or action can ever be traced more deeply than to this point; no cause can ever be defined which underlies it: it is the root cause, the deepest source of all outflow in the mind and *neshama*. In fact, if one can generate the ruthless honesty required for this exercise, when one traces one's motivation down to the underlying desire which subsumes all the more superficial desires, that one all-encompassing desire is an accurate definition of *who one is* essentially. Each motivation has a reason, a goal — if I could achieve this, it would lead to that, and so on. But ultimately the one final *tachlis* (purpose) to which all the others lead, the one which has no ulterior element, that which one wants *because one wants it* — that is the source.

This deep root is the tool of *bechira* (free will); one can begin to understand why *bechira* is expressed as the crowning glory of the human, the very *tzelem Elokim*, "image of G-d" element in the human structure. Free will is precisely the function of the source dimension, nothing conditions or forces a really *free* choice. This is also the secret behind what is meant by the *"ratzon Hashem"*, the Divine will; it is the ultimate source.

Not only is this area of *ratzon* the root of the personality; in a certain sense it is the entire personality: once an active desire exists all else in the personality is no more than machinery, mechanisms for implementing that desire. A close analogy is the way a physical action is performed: once the brain has generated the nerve impulse which passes down the nerves to the muscles causing the action, the process is automatic. The nerve and muscle functions are mechanical; animals are no different, and even a machine could duplicate those components of the process. The *only* part which is uniquely human is the initial *generating of the idea* which results in mechanical function. In terms of meaning, that is everything. Ali the rest is technical. Meaningful change can only be a change at the level of will, the level of human decision concerning which acts to perform. Changes in the mechanics — which muscles are to be used and how, for example, are insignificant; these are simply variations in the means.

Similarly, any changes made superficially in the personality are really only changes in strategy: how to go about achieving the same end in a different way. The only truly meaningful change must be a change in the root. The technical machinery of the mind and body are slaves to the goal, the *ratzon*. It is all too easy to make changes superficially; often these changes reflect a stubborn and very effective method of avoiding confrontation with the core, the "real you". Spiritual growth requires that confrontation, difficult though it may be. The battle is to fight through to one's own core, to acknowledge it and lay it bare, to reach that interface with the Root of the *neshama* which is beyond it and which animates and inspires it.

II. DESIRE AND THE DEPTH OF PRAYER

The exercise which most directly develops this contact with the root of desire is *tefilla*, prayer. In order to understand this, let us ask some fundamental questions about prayer.

There are aspects of prayer which seem to defy explanation. Our prayers are phrased as requests. We ask the Creator for our needs; this is an essential element of prayer. The difficulty is, how can we hope to achieve anything by asking? Surely Hashem knows what we need before we ask, and being a loving Father, surely He will give us our needs even if we do not ask? And conversely, surely He would not grant our requests if the consequences would be negative for us; so what difference can our asking possibly make? Put differently, how can we hope to change Hashem's mind, as it were? If He has decided that a certain thing is to be, how can we convince Him otherwise? If we could effect some change, somehow, that would be nothing less than miraculous.

If we cannot make any difference then, by praying, why do we do it? Are we really expected to pour out our hearts in deeply-felt pleading while knowing that our pleas can have no effect? Why in fact are our prayers expressed as requests at all — if prayer is a meditation, a spiritual communion, it would seem that personal requests are an inappropriate medium; surely depersonalized concentration would be better? And if prayer is service, asking for our needs seems quite the opposite.

There are other paradoxical aspects of prayer. The word תפלה *tefilla*, prayer, is based on a root which has two opposite meanings: פלל has the connotation of the hope of completely unpredictable, illogical consequences occurring, great kindness being expressed despite circumstances suggesting otherwise, as it says *"Re'o panecha lo pillalti* — I could not have hoped to see your face again", the words of Yaakov's wonder at seeing Yosef after so many years of separation. Yet the same root means strict, deserved justice — פללי connotes justice in the narrow legal sense, exactly the opposite of unexpected bounty. How are these conflicting elements contained in prayer?

Perhaps an even deeper problem is this: the *gemara* states quite plainly that Hashem *davens* (prays). Hashem Himself, the One who has the power to grant all requests, the source and definition of all reality, praying? We are forced to ask incredulously: to whom? How is it possible to understand this statement at all?

*   *   *

Let us begin with a wonderful answer to the first set of questions we asked, those which pose the problem of somehow changing Hashem, an obvious impossibility. The key to this issue is to understand that prayer is *not* directed at changing Hashem at all; it is directed at changing *you*. The idea is that the work of *tefilla* (prayer is known as *avoda she'b'lev* — the *work* of the heart) is work on the self, the effort to change the personality. It has been said that if one takes three steps backwards at the end of *shmone esrei* (eighteen-fold prayer central to the prayer service) and is not a different person, one has failed in that *tefilla*. Work on the personality means making changes; some refinement, some elevation must occur.

Now let us apply this idea to some of the specifics we mentioned: the reason we hope to achieve a result through *tefilla*, to make some change in the world or our situation in it, is as follows. We certainly cannot convince Hashem that we need some or other particular thing if He knows otherwise. However we can change ourselves to the point that the object of our request has a different meaning: if a person wants wealth, for example, and is being refused that request because *it would not be good for him* (wealth can be a great ordeal), no amount of pleading will change that. But working on oneself until one reaches a refinement, an insight into the purpose of life and the correct perspective on wealth could result in a situation where that gift may now be *good* for the person! In other words one *can* change the dispensation granted to one by changing oneself! A new dispensation now becomes appropriate. So we see that *tefilla* is not just a meditation, a communion; it is most certainly intended to produce results too. Of course it is immediately apparent that the work of *tefilla* is not simply asking for things, it must be very hard and sincere work indeed to change oneself genuinely.

(The very first change which occurs is in one's relationship with Hashem. The act of asking itself puts one in correct perspective: one asks for a thing only from that which one believes to be a valid source of that thing. This change alone can result in one's receiving something which one would not have received otherwise; the first element which Hashem desires from our *tefilla* is that we put ourselves in a position of asking. We thereby acknowledge the source; this automatically implies that we will appreciate Hashem as the source when a subsequent request is granted. In analogy: a father may be ready and willing to give his child some particular thing, but he may be withholding it because his prime objective may be the relationship between himself and his child — if the child were to consciously acknowledge his father as the giver that may be all the father is waiting for.)

*   *   *

Before dealing with the other questions which we raised, let us focus on the nature of this change. As mentioned earlier, a real change in the personality must be a change in *ratzon*. Only a change in the root, the *tachlis* dimension, can be considered meaningful, all else is only technical re-arranging of the superficial. How does one change one's *ratzon*? How does one "bring in" a new desire? This issue is pivotal.

The first phase of *tefilla* is to reach the *ratzon*, to "ascend" in the consciousness until one penetrates into the very core of one's own personality. To stand facing one's own root desire, that distilled essence from which flows all the rest of one's inner life and outer behavior, and to face it honestly and unafraid, is an absolute requirement for genuine change. This is a very high meditation indeed. All superficial thoughts must be banished, intense concentration is needed.

But far more difficult to understand is: when one finally reaches that depth, how is a change made? How do you create a new desire? How do you sincerely come to want that which is higher, more refined, more spiritual, if you do not want it now? To put this into more mystical terms: you cannot go "up" outside of yourself and bring down a new desire; the most that can be done, surely, is to experience the root of what you are — but where is the ladder to climb higher? Simply to *say* that you want something else would be a lie; it must be felt, known, more deeply than anything else.

The solution is that one cannot cause a new *ratzon* to be manifest; by definition *ratzon* is the root cause, it cannot be brought about as a result of some other cause. Put simply, your deepest *ratzon* level is *you*, that cannot be voluntarily changed.

You cannot do it; but Hashem can! A change of the deepest essence of the self, an elevation of that essence, is a gift! We have referred to this in another context previously — the climb to the top is work; going beyond that top is a gift. It comes from outside of the self — a new level, a new sensitivity; that is the ultimate gift, that is the answer to prayer!

(Although one cannot voluntarily create a new desire, there is one thing which can be felt powerfully in a natural way: the desire to change! One cannot lie and say: I want this or that more selfless level, but one *can* say: Hashem, I really do want to have a higher *ratzon*, I *want* to feel a higher desire! *I want to want it!* One should pour one's heart out in the request to be elevated.)

How does one merit this gift? If it comes from above the self, how can one bring it down? The answer is that in order for that *shefa*, that flow of Divine energy to fill the *neshama* (soul), one must become a vessel for it. The flow is there, the only question is where are the vessels? Hashem's desire to give is maximal and permanent, but where are we? (A wonderful hint to this lies in the miraculous blessing brought about by Elisha for the poor woman: Elisha instructed her to bring vessels and the oil flowed miraculously to fill the vessels — until there were no more vessels! There is no problem with the oil; the limitation is only in the vessels.)

What does it mean to become a vessel? How exactly is this done? There is a mystical idea that the highest level of the personality is crystal-clear and transparent, but the lower self, the ego, clouds it. (Spiritual beauty is expressed as being transparent, Hashem's light shines through. When one sees a *tzaddik* (righteous individual) one is perceiving something of Hashem; the limited human dimension has been clarified and a higher reality becomes visible. In fact the opposite of beauty, ugliness, is כעור, the same root letters as עכור, opaque.)

An analogy lies in thought: concentration applied to solve a problem does *not* mean focusing on the solution to the problem — one does not *have* the solution to focus on; concentration simply means clearing the mind of extraneous thoughts, keeping mental "noise" out of the way, clearing a space in the mind as it were, and the solution appears *by itself!* An idea is not created — it appears! In Yiddish an "idea" is an *"einfal"*: it *falls in*. Of course!

The stronger the lower side of the personality, the vested interests, the selfish, the more clouded the *ratzon*-dimension becomes. The paradox of spiritual living is that to become greater, more real, one has to give up the lower desires which clamor so aggressively for attention. The greatest man who ever lived, Moshe, was also the most humble — no accident; being humble was the *reason* for his greatness: when the self is emptied, Hashem can fill it! Our work is not to cause the light to shine, only to stop obstructing it. To paraphrase the comment of a sage: the world is full of light; we cast the shadows.

*   *   *

The spiritual path is always a paradox — real honor finds only those who flee from it (really flee — a man once complained to the Chazon Ish that he had fled from honor all his life and it had still not found him! The Chazon Ish gently chided him: "You have been too busy looking over your shoulder!") Real content is found only in those who are really empty.

Put in *ratzon* terms, this clarifying process means *yielding* all one's *ratzon* to Hashem. This is the meaning of *"Aseh retzoncha retzono* — Make your will His will", give up your will so that you want what He wants! This does *not* mean becoming a passive, lifeless individual; on the contrary, one must *passionately* want what Hashem wants! This level is given as a gift to the degree that one gains control over one's own negative drives and interests.

So the meditation and the work of *tefilla* is to identify one's deepest core and then to yield it. In effect one is saying: "Hashem, this is who I am. This is *everything* that I am; all meaning in my life is concentrated here, in my deepest desire. Take it, Hashem, and do with it as You see fit. I give myself to You."

Actually, this is the secret of Torah living in general; in *tefilla* it is made explicit.

The paradox of *tefilla* which requires the most work is yielding *ratzon* and simultaneously building *ratzon*. One controls one's own desires until they are not felt, and then concentrates on amplifying the higher *ratzon* which results. And yet, at the same time one allows one's desires to be richly felt and then sublimates them into service of Hashem.

This explains, too, why our *tefillos* are composed of requests, desires expressed. That is exactly the medium of prayer; prayer is the work of changing desires! The work of prayer is work on *ratzon*. The Nefesh Hachaim explains this as follows. We phrase our prayers as requests because we are working on our *ratzon*, but when we ask for all the things which we mention in the *tefilla*, we should be asking for those things for Hashem, not for us! We use our desire, but for Him. Give us wisdom — for Your service, Hashem. Give us health — to perform Your *mitzvos*. And so on. A remarkable exercise of self-development, using our potentially selfish motivations to sublimate those very motivations to a higher purpose! Of course some thought will show that it has to be this way: standing before Hashem with a list of personal requests all for completely selfish reasons would be a *chutzpa* (effrontery) — that is not service!

The Nefesh Hachaim points out that we learn many of the aspects and details of *tefilla* from Chana's prayer — when she came to the Sanctuary and prayed for a child. What the Nefesh Hachaim states briefly we can understand in more detail. We are told that Chana prayed very powerfully, even somehow going beyond the apparent limits of what should be said. The Beis Halevi explains that she went so far as to threaten extreme action in order to get her way — she told Hashem that if He refused her request for a child she would seclude herself with a man other than her husband and cause herself to be subjected to the test of a *sotah* (woman suspected of unfaithfulness to her husband) in which Hashem's name is erased into water. When the suspected *sotah* drinks the water the result depends on the truth of her behavior: if she is guilty, she suffers a miserable end, but if she is innocent she becomes pregnant and gives birth — a promise of the Torah. Chana used this stratagem: "Hashem, I intend to do this. Since I shall be innocent, You will *have* to give me a child — You have promised thus in Your Torah and You will never make Your Torah untrue!" Forcing the Divine hand! A sharp prayer indeed.

But the meaning is clear, as the Nefesh Hachaim explains: Chana was motivated only for Hashem's honor and glory. The intensity of her prayer was really: Hashem, by undergoing the test of the *sotah* I shall definitely have a child. But I am asking You for a child without having to go through that experience because that would mean erasing Your name! Allow me the inevitable result without such a desecration of Your honor! And we see how sincere she was: the child she was granted was dedicated to Hashem from the earliest possible age — she presented her son Shmuel (Samuel) to the *mishkan* (Sanctuary) to be raised in Hashem's service for the rest of his life. Her very *desire* for this child in the first place was dedicated to Hashem; she wanted a son *for Hashem's sake* — she sublimated her desire to be a mother to *avodas Hashem*, service of Hashem.

How fitting the name she gave that son born of her prayer: Shmuel, "Hashem hears". The perfect source for the Jewish people to learn the laws of *tefilla* — a Jewish woman using her own desire to be a mother for Hashem's service entirely.

*　*　*

Perhaps now we can understand the paradox of the פלל root of the word *tefilla:* the strict line of destiny and yet combined with the almost unbelievable kindness of unexpected results — Hashem wants to give, *intends* to give, but He waits for our *tefilla*. He waits for us to make our *ratzon* His *ratzon*. He makes His desire to give dependent on our desire to receive. When we *ask*, He reveals what must be. The result occurs *only* because we ask, and yet it is a revelation of Hashem's will.

We can best understand this from its source in Torah: the *midrashic* sources say that when Adam was created, he did not see a garden. The vegetation and foliage of the garden were not present; growth had stopped at the surface of the ground because there was no rain. And there was no rain because *"Va'adam ayin la'avod es ha'adama* — There was no man to work the land"; the word "work" is a reference to work of the heart — prayer. In other words, since no-one was present to pray, there was no rain. If Adam does not *ask* for rain, there will be no rain. Despite the fact that the rain is waiting, poised, a necessary part of Creation, it *will not be* if man does not express his desire for it. And when he does ask for it, the garden of Eden is revealed *as it had to be*.

The rain is one of the few things in the Creation which Hashem Himself causes directly, not through any agent. This means that the Torah is teaching us most profoundly that the response to our *tefillos* is the deepest response imaginable — Hashem Himself is waiting for us to activate the partnership. And the result is rain, life-giving rain.

We see here a source at the very beginning of the world for the essential nature of *tefilla*. Not a nicety, an option, but an absolute requirement. The result is a harmony of Divine and human will which builds the world, literally. And perhaps that gives us an added depth in understanding *"Kol milin d'alma lo talyin ela b're'usa* — Everything in the world depends on desire".

* * *

Can we now venture an insight into the gemara's statement that Hashem prays? We have defined *tefilla* in essence as a change in *ratzon*. What is Hashem's *tefilla*? The *gemara* states that Hashem prays as follows: "May it be My will to arise from the throne of justice and move to the throne of mercy." *Yehi ratzon mil'fanai...* May it be *My will!* We are being taught that at the very source of the world an act of prayer is an act of changing *ratzon*, will. And just as He says *"Yehi ratzon mil'fanai...*May it be My will", we say *"Yehi ratzon mil'fanecha...* May it be Your will..."

So prayer is a breakthrough into the root of the personality to connect with the Root of the world. When we make that connection Hashem pours His energy into us and the world.

How do we make that connection? By opening our hearts entirely, conquering the opacifying effects of petty desires and lower drives. By *becoming* that desire to manifest Hashem's desire. And who better to learn from than David, the one who comes to teach absolute control of the ego, to reveal Hashem's *malchus*, kingship, in the world through his own kingship. David, the great singer of songs to Hashem who will one day be manifest in the *mashiach*, in dedication of every fiber of his being to Hashem says of himself *"Va'ani tefilla"* — not "I pray", but "I *am* prayer"!

Chapter 10

Intellect and Imagination

L et us turn to the outer mind. Just as the *da'as* (inner knowledge) has a root level which is higher, namely *ratzon* (will or desire), so too the outer mind is composed of two levels. These can be grasped as *sechel*, intellect, and *dimyon*, imagination. All the aspects of primary or root levels and their relationship with secondary or outer levels apply here too. Just as in the phases of experience there is a higher source of inspiration and a more difficult phase which follows; just as in the *da'as* there is an inspired, higher source called *ratzon*, so too *sechel* is a higher layer and *dimyon* a lower one in the outer mind. Let us trace their interaction in order to understand something very deep and fundamental about the harmony of the mind. Contained in this discussion is an essential key to mind control and the power of concentration.

All male and female or abstract-plan and concrete-building pairs consist of the same basic elements. Let us define them and then apply them to the *sechel-dimyon* relationship. The plan or code level is abstract but contains all the instructions needed for the physical level to do all that it must do (just as the genes which the father gives contain all that is needed for the mother to actually form the child). The abstract level lacks energy. All the power for physical building is contributed by the mother on the more physical level. The abstract level is all theory, the physical level is all tangible reality. One without the other is useless: a plan with no builder remains theory. A builder with no plan will build a haphazard, illogical mess. Together a meaningful, well-planned and well-executed result is achieved.

The Maharal expresses this relationship as that between form and substance. Form is an abstract concept, substance is tangible. The form imposes itself upon the substance, so the substance has a form. All substance must have *some* form; all form must have *some* substance to express it. Harmony is achieved when the substance most appropriately, most beautifully expresses its form. This is the depth of understanding of all art and esthetics.

How does all this express itself in *sechel* and *dimyon,* intellect and imagination?

The intellect is pure theory. It is the set of instructions, the logical pathways which the mind uses to think. It is pure form, pure abstract logic. The imagination is the set of graphic images which the mind contains and constructs which provide the *substance* which thought manipulates. If you like, the intellect is the computer program, the imagination is the specific information which must be given to the computer for the program to run. The intellect is the logic of the mathematical equation; the imagination is the set of specific numbers which that equation contains.

Intellect has no innate energy; imagination does. When one

leans back in an easy chair and relaxes, intellect does not function, imagination does. Intellect must be specifically motivated, intended. To develop a logical train of thought one must intend it and work at it. To experience wild imagination, one has only to still the logical.

Even more than this: it is extremely difficult to maintain prolonged logical thinking, in fact it is extremely difficult to concentrate on one subject for any length of time. What usually happens (and usually when one least wants it!) is that in the middle of a logical thought pattern some extraneous imagination image swells in the mind, and in a flash a series of associations takes place which leaves one dreaming about something so far removed from what one began with that one cannot even remember how one got there!

One has only to attempt an intense *shmone esrei* (eighteen-fold prayer central to prayer service) to realise how difficult it is to maintain rigorously logical, productive, ordered thought.

The reason for this problem is that intellect is passive — it must be driven, but imagination is full of energy — it runs by itself. Since by definition imagination is all graphic images, memories, pictures, and has *no logic* of its own, its associations are haphazard and illogical. And since all power is vested in the imagination, it is connected to the emotions and the basic drives of the personality; it has all the energy needed for building, making tangible — it runs away uncontrolled whenever it is allowed to.

The path is painfully familiar: you move from step "A" to step "B" in a logical thought sequence, trying to solve a problem, let us say, or to make a plan for some important event. Hardly have you reached "B" when some peripheral, irrelevant detail of "B" stimulates a powerful memory (a graphic, energy-filled element of the imagination). That memory, purely by association, triggers another. Some peripheral detail of *that* memory triggers yet another image, picture, memory. And again, you are lost in a reverie so intense that you have forgotten the present and the problem you set out to solve. In irritation and frustration you shake out of the dream and start again on your train of logical thought. Until the next rapid-fire burst of distraction.

This is all too familiar to each one of us. It is a rare person who has built the self-discipline to think powerfully on one subject for even a few minutes at a time without distraction.

The secret is to bring the imagination under the control of the intellect. *Dimyon* must serve *sechel*. *Sechel* must inform, direct *dimyon*. The intellect must call up from the imagination *only* those elements — images, memories, facts — which are needed for this step of the thought process and *no more*. When the step is completed, those graphic elements must be suppressed and the next set called up. The imagination must never over-supply the intellect, never intrude with all its richness of memory, image and emotion. That harmony is thought control. That is concentration.

This harmony takes various forms. A great creative artist, for example, will allow free rein to the imagination. Almost free: the intellect will provide just enough control so that there is a unity of theme to the creative stream, a balance, an esthetic connection. The balance will be that of an immensely powerful horse directed by a small but highly sensitive and skilled rider. On the other hand, a powerful mathematician will force logic to dominate entirely. Almost entirely: the logic will need facts, figures, numbers to give it just enough tangible form to proceed.

This is the analysis of thought. Understanding it can be a profoundly significant factor in developing concentration. The goal is a perfect marriage; perfect harmony between the abstract form and the tangible substance, between the abstract root of logic in the mind and the graphic expression of imagination. That harmony of opposites is real beauty.

Chapter 11

Beauty and the Source of Shame

We have studied the relationship between *ratzon* (desire) and *da'as* (knowledge), and between *sechel* (intellect) and *dimyon* (imagination).

Let us attempt to understand the relationship between *neshama* (soul) and *guf* (body). We have seen the connection between inspiration and application of that inspiration, or root and outgrowth of that root from a number of perspectives. How does the root, the *neshama*, express itself in the physical, the body? What is the nature of the tension between these two? How does this tension become a harmony? Many wonderful secrets are contained in this area.

As one moves down from the more spiritual to the more physical levels, tension or disharmony between the inner core and the outer vessels becomes more apparent. The physical or outer layers begin to pull away, to rebel; the perfect relationship of inner plan and outer building tends to break down. Maintaining harmony becomes a more challenging task. In the relationship between *neshama* and body, this problem becomes acute. Let us probe this as deeply as we are able.

Like all pairs of inner form and outer matter, the pair of *neshama* and body should be in perfect balance. The body should reflect the *neshama* perfectly, should serve it in perfect loyalty. Never should the body stray after its own desires. It should be a vessel, a tool which obeys its control dimension totally selflessly. It should be a vehicle driven only from within, its very existence justified only as a loyal servant.

At the Creation, the body of Adam was just that. It was an ethereal, luminescent structure which revealed the spiritual content. Adam reached from earth to heaven, and glowed with purity. The *gemara* states that even in death the light which shone from his heels was brighter than the sun. His beauty was indescribable. Adam and Chava (Eve) were pure people in pure bodies. And most significantly, they wore no clothes and were not ashamed. *"Va'yiheyu shneihem arumim ha'adam ve'ishto ve'lo yisboshashu* — And the two of them were naked, the man and his wife, and they were not ashamed."

When the inner reality is perfectly reflected in the outer, when the spirituality of the *neshama* animates and energizes the body so that it glows visibly, shame is not possible. Shame is the pain of a human mind betrayed by a body; a core which is angelic deserves to be clothed like an angel — when the clothing looks animal, shame is inevitable. Shame is the result of a breakdown between inner and outer dimensions. Truth and beauty demand that the inside is represented accurately on the outside. When the outside betrays the inside it demeans and shames it most intensely.

Let us understand. When Adam and Chava were created

they were not ashamed because the vessels of their bodies perfectly reflected their *neshamos*. The body was faithful to the *neshama* entirely. But sin changed all that. Sin was a surrender to the body. Sin made the human a part of physicality instead of remaining in his proper relationship to the physical — above it. With their sin, Adam and Chava crashed to the lowest level of the physical universe and became subject to the material instead of remaining masters of it. An angelic core is condemned to move in a body indistinguishable from an animal — that is shame. Adam and Chava felt the most acute shame imaginable in their lowered state, and they were aware that they had caused it — that is the real heart of shame.

The body had been allowed to speak, and it had taken over entirely. No longer was it a faithful servant, it had become a master.

*   *   *

Breakdown between inner and outer. This is the source of all moral pain. The idea of שקר falsehood, is the same. Speech, communication, should reveal the hidden. Its function is to reveal outwardly that which is secret in the mind. When it does so, it is a faithful tool. But when the words lie, when the tool of expression is used to *misrepresent* what is inward, it has become treacherous. Treachery is the immorality of using outward garb to mislead. A traitor wears clothing which misrepresents the wearer, a "turncoat" indeed. True expression connects the inner and outer worlds accurately, connects two minds accurately. Lies break down the connection between inner and outer, treacherously. This is the immorality of lying. The word שקר a lie, is a re-arrangement of קשר connection. Of course.

The response to shame, the expression of shame, is to hide. Adam covered his nakedness, and hid. Part of the reason for his hiding in the Garden was shame. As we have noted previously, a garment in Hebrew is בגד the root of treachery. Another word for clothing is לבוש; there are sources which state that this word is mystically an acronym of לא בוש — "not ashamed", that is, prevention of shame. But there is more to clothing than this. Clothes hide but also reveal — although the wearer is hidden by his clothes, his dignity is revealed by his clothes. Royal robes cover the king, but they reveal his royalty. *("Oteh or ka'salma* — Hashem wears light like a *garment"; nature hides Hashem, but accurately reveals His presence!)*

The response to a fallen state, a state of shame, is to use clothes correctly: to cover nakedness, but to reveal dignity. To cover the animal, but to reveal the human at the same time. To use the article of failure for redemption itself! Hashem taught Adam this lesson by *making* him proper clothes in addition to the minimal covering of leaves which he had taken himself — there is more to clothing than covering.

The mystics explain these ideas more deeply. The garments of the world, the covering of Adam before he sinned were of אור — "light". After the sin, the covering became עור — "skin" or "hide" (appropriate word!) The root אור has the silent "א", it is light, spiritual, all revelation. The root עור spells not only skin but *blind* too — the covering which revealed has become a covering which obstructs.

*   *   *

The result of the sin was the tension between *neshama* and body, between spirituality and materialism. The two were created to be in harmony, partners, now they are at war. The body which had been an avenue to the spiritual has become a distraction. When one expands, the other shrinks. Before one can develop spiritually, become more sensitive, the physical must be controlled. If one stimulates the physical, the spiritual is dulled. The relationship which was to be complementary has become inverse. He who wishes to learn Torah must learn to discipline his material nature. In turn, as Torah content increases in the personality, the physical becomes tamed.

The *gemara* teaches this inverse relationship in a striking way. Rabbi Yehoshua ben Chananya was once engaged in conversation by a Roman princess. Rabbi Yehoshua was *"chakima d'Yehudai* — the wise man of the Jews", a giant of a sage who defended the Jews of his generation in forced debates against outsiders. Apart from his legendary greatness in learning, what was outstanding about him was his ugliness. He was so strikingly ugly in fact, that the princess was moved to ask him how such great wisdom could be contained in such a lowly vessel.

He replied "In what does your father keep his wine?"

"In earthenware vessels", she answered.

Caesar kept his wine in earthenware jars like everyone else.

"Is that fitting for a king?" said Rabbi Yehoshua. "Surely a king should store his wine in gold and silver vessels!"

Caesar's daughter agreed. She returned to the palace and ordered all her father's wine transferred to gold and silver containers. Of course, the alcohol in the wine leached the metal out of the containers and the wine became sour. When Caesar tasted the wine he demanded an explanation. His daughter said "Rabbi Yehoshua ben Chananya told me to do it!"

Caesar called for Rabbi Yehoshua. "What is going on here?" he asked.

Answered Rabbi Yehoshua "I simply answered her according to her question. I wished to show her that when the vessel becomes important, it spoils the contents." Profound words!

This exchange must be analyzed. It is not accidental that the question was asked by a Roman and a woman. Rome held the legacy of Greece, and at the center of that cultural legacy was the idea of esthetics. Beautiful contents demand beautiful containers — that is the essence of esthetics, of art. And it is woman who is responsible for the expression of beauty. She, a Roman woman, was unable to reconcile great and beautiful wisdom in a lowly container, a misshapen body.

Rabbi Yehoshua taught her that in the world of spiritual values, the two are locked in mortal battle. The container must be simple for the contents to be pure. Only when the vessel is humble does it not detract from what it holds — Moshe was the greatest man who ever lived, who contained the entirety of Torah, *because he was the most humble*.

The *gemara* records that the conversation did not end there. Caesar's daughter was not yet convinced by Rabbi Yehoshua's answer.

"What about your colleagues?" she asked, referring to the fact that some of the great sages of Judaism were extremely beautiful! (Rabbi Yochanan once visited a friend who was ill and due to his poverty lay in darkness. Rabbi Yochanan rolled up his sleeve and *lit the house* with the incandescence of his beauty. His one exposed forearm was sufficient!) So Caesar's daughter was perplexed: if ugliness is a prerequisite for wisdom, why are some sages beautiful *and* wise?

Replied Rabbi Yehoshua "Had they been ugly, they would have been much wiser!" Despite the disadvantage of physical beauty, they achieved wisdom!

* * *

We learn, therefore, that a most powerful way to increase spiritual depth is to control the physical. This is the essence of *tznius*, that profound modesty which is the domain of Jewish women. In woman, physical beauty is striking, sensual. If uncontrolled, projected as animal, the spiritual withers and wilts. The special and sacred task of Jewish woman is to present the physical in such a way that the *neshama* shines through. Exposing the body as fashion may dictate, expressing the body with deportment which is physical — these lead to a loss of refinement, a profaning of the holy. A most important rule is that the spiritual flourishes *because* it is hidden. The real beauty of woman in Jewish terms lies in deep privacy, in guarding morality.

Yosef, the only man in *Chumash* who is described as beautiful in terms usually used for woman, was the one who resisted immorality in superhuman fashion. The two go together.

* * *

Inner, spiritual values are inversely related to outer, physical ones. This principle applies on many levels; pathways in the spiritual are opposite to pathways in the physical. In the spiritual world, for example, things improve with time: wisdom increases with age if nurtured correctly. But in the physical, things degrade, decay with time: the body deteriorates with age no matter how carefully nurtured. The physical is the zone of contact with evil, with death-forces — it is subject to these forces and its pathway is negative, from strength to disintegration. The spiritual is the zone of contact with a higher reality — its pathway is positive, from weaker to stronger.

All things in the physical world get worn down with time, get worse with time. Except wine! It is no accident that Rabbi Yehoshua's graphic lesson to the Roman princess (and to us) was taught with wine. Wine is the physical creation which provides a window into the hidden world; it reveals secrets and it obeys the rules of the hidden world. Wine in Hebrew is יין whose numerical equivalent is סוד "secret". And hence *"Nichnas yayin yatza sod* — When wine goes in, the secret comes out". Wine has the capacity to reveal secrets in more ways than one.

Wine has the paradoxical capacity to dehumanize, to make one who uses it to excess part of the physical; and yet if used correctly, it has the capacity to elevate, to sensitize consciousness. A physical substance, yet with connection to the spiritual.

This insight leads to an understanding of a special depth in the Jewish path to inner growth. Our path, our Torah method of correcting the problem of the tension between spiritual and physical, is to connect the two in such a way that the spiritual elevates the physical. We use the physical, but only as a vehicle for the spiritual. And that is why we take wine at occasions of connecting the two: at a wedding, where two physical bodies will elevate their relationship to the spiritual; at a *bris,* circumcision, where we begin the process of sanctifying the body; at *kiddush,* where the more physical domain of the week meets the transcendence of Shabbos; at the Pesach *seder,* where slavery transitions to freedom.

That is our path, to generate harmony between the inner and outer worlds; not to reject the physical (that is much easier) but to bring it under control of the spiritual; to train the body into absolute loyalty to the *neshama.* That harmony of opposites is beauty, it is the cure for shame. And that must be our path until the end of history, when the body and the physical will again become the spiritually glowing vessels they were created to be.

III.

Structure
of
Time

Chapter 12

Time

We have learned that our experience in life takes shape in phases — inspiration, loss of inspiration, and the battle to regain inspiration. We have seen that the fabric of our minds and *neshamos* contains elements which correspond to these phases. Let us delve into the nature of time itself in order to discover the root of these energies. The result of becoming sensitive to time in this way is the ability to harmonize the mind and *neshama* elements with the time elements — to ride the waves of time.

The overall vessel which contains the rest of Creation is time. This medium of time is not monotonous and one-dimensional; it flows in cycles which have pulsations of energy. These cycles correspond exactly to the various energy-levels we have mentioned in the human dimension, or rather, they constitute the framework or container of the human dimension; we exist within time and resonate with it. If we can learn to feel the flow of these time-cycles we can "tune" our spiritual energy appropriately and amplify immeasurably our spiritual growth.

Time cycles through units of moments, hours, days, weeks, months and years. In fact, the cycles are really spirals because no two moments are ever identical — each re-visiting of a point in time is really corresponding but higher; the work demanded is to "correct" or energize each point correctly, no point ever presents itself twice and therefore each day of a human life, each moment in fact, needs specific spiritual effort. The Nefesh Hachaim explains that *shacharis* (morning prayer) today is entirely different from *shacharis* tomorrow — today is not tomorrow and it needs its own special work. The same words tomorrow have an entirely new effect. These points in time are our most valuable commodity –– our lives, in fact.

Put more clearly, each moment is charged with the energy to help us achieve what we need to achieve *at that moment;* time is not the passive matrix on which we imprint our actions, it is the *energy source for those actions.*

Let us study this idea. We often understand that we celebrate the anniversary of certain events, for example, because we remember that those events occurred at those particular times and thereby made the times special — we celebrate Pesach in spring because the Exodus occurred then. Actually, the opposite is true. The truth is that the Exodus occurred then because the mystical forces of time made it possible, even necessary, then: time is a cause, not an onlooker. One has only to remember that Avraham Avinu ate *matza* at Pesach time although in his generation there was no Exodus to commemorate, not even a Jewish people on the scene yet. The energies of that time of year demand *matza*, demand Pesach. The observances of Pesach commemorate the Exodus, it is true, but that Exodus itself with all its details is an expression of the energies inherent in time.

And so it is with every Yom Tov, every day in fact. This is the deeper meaning of *"Ba'yamim ha'hem ba'zman ha'zeh* — "In those days, at this time" — at this time of year an energy equivalent to that which pulsated in the world then is present; our task is not to commemorate it sentimentally but to *use it*.

We understand therefore, that a year is a circle whose points are unique. Each point on that circle is immensely powerful, generates waves of energy which make certain events and attainments possible *at that point*. Each point demands certain efforts from us, individually and as a people. Each individual lifetime is a circle or spiral; *each day of our lives* demands a certain sensitivity, a certain growth, a specific achievement. There are moments of opportunity which never appear twice. This is also the deeper meaning of the section in *Koheles* (Ecclesiastes) which states that "To everything there is a season, and a time to every purpose...."

* * *

Let us study the uniqueness of each moment's opportunity. The *gemara* recounts what follows Moshe Rabbeinu's request to Hashem to show him more of Hashem's glory, of His presence. Hashem refuses, saying that Moshe cannot see more.

We can imagine Moshe's response: "But when I stood at the burning bush, Hashem, You *offered* to show me and I was too afraid to look. Now that I feel able to look, I beg of You to reveal more."

The *gemara* records Hashem's reply: *"K'she'ratzisi, lo ratzisa; achshav she'ata rotzeh, eini rotzeh* — When I wanted to reveal

Myself to you, you did not want it. Now that you want, I do not." The *gemara* there records an opinion that when Moshe hid his face previously and was afraid to look he did nothing wrong. His behavior was appropriate and praiseworthy. This is not a punishment. *But that was the time,* and you missed it. This is not the time. What a lesson in missed opportunities!

Shir Hashirim (Song of Songs) states: "I am sleeping but my heart is awake; (I hear) the sound of my beloved knocking: Open for me my sister, my beloved, my dove, my pure one.... I had taken off my cloak, should I put it on again? I had washed my feet, should I soil them?" And then, after delaying: "I arose to open for my beloved, but my beloved was gone...." A brief laziness — an opportunity lost. That knock at the door must be answered.

It seems that a person must develop an exquisite sensitivity to the energy flow of time — must know what can be achieved when. The mystics talk about this in detail. The students of the great Arizal, the kabbalist who lived in Tzefas over four hundred years ago, record that late one *erev* Shabbos, Friday afternoon, as they stood with their master in the hills of Tzefas to greet the Shabbos, he turned to them suddenly and said "Let us go to Yerushalayim." They were stunned — there were only moments to sundown and Yerushalayim is a long way from Tzefas. He obviously meant that they would be transported there above time, perhaps even meant something much greater would happen than that they would simply arrive in Yerushalayim. There was a moment's hesitation in the group — someone said something about just telling his family — and the Arizal said sadly "It is too late".

The great *talmid* (disciple) of the Arizal, Rabbi Chaim Vital, records the following event in his writings. After his master's passing he was in Yerushalayim. One day the Sultan of Yerushalayim approached him and ordered him to open the waters of the Gichon. The Gichon was an underground spring which flowed inside Yerushalayim and which had been sealed by King Chizkiyahu, as the *gemara* records, against the wishes of the sages of his generation.

We understand that the sealing or unsealing of these waters has far deeper significance than the simply technical, but let us note at least the superficial level for the present. The Sultan knew that the great kabbalist Rabbi Chaim Vital would have the mystical power to unseal the long-sealed spring. Rabbi Vital was afraid to comply but knew that his life was in danger if he refused, and he therefore used a certain kabbalistic technique to transport himself instantaneously to Damascus.

That night his Rebbe, the Arizal, appeared to him in a dream.

"Why did you refuse to open the Gichon today?" he asked his *talmid*.

"I was afraid to use the holy names of Hashem which would have been necessary for that", answered Reb Chaim.

"And how did you get to Damascus?"

Obviously, Reb Chaim had no reply to that. Then the Arizal said:

"Do you know that your soul is a *gilgul* (re-incarnation) of King Chizkiyahu and that you were *brought to the world* to re-open that spring after sealing it so many years ago?"

We can imagine Reb Chaim's feelings. He writes that he responded by saying "I shall go back tomorrow and do it."

Said the Arizal "You cannot do that. *Today was the day* and the opportunity is gone."

Although it is not our business to delve into these

marvelous depths too deeply, we see in a startling way the unique power of a specific time. It seems that one of our special ordeals is to use our opportunities correctly. We dare not miss the moment. But we cannot be *"dochek es hasha'a* — force the hour" either; too soon is as invalid as too late. The people of Ephraim left Egypt ahead of the rest of the Jewish people convinced that the redemption-time had arrived. They were wrong, and were decimated as a result. Timing is the secret.

*   *   *

How does one know which is the moment? How does one become sensitive to one's opportunities? We understand that Hashem never gives us difficulties too profound for us to utilize; if we are meant to use an opportunity we will be given a sufficient hint, each according to his or her sensitivity. For the highly developed the hint may be subtle: when Elisha was a young man plowing his father's fields on a particular day, Eliyahu (Elijah) the great prophet and leader of the generation passed close by him. As he passed, he cast his cloak over Elisha. That was enough. Elisha bade his parents farewell and followed the man who had just become his master; and went on to become a prophet and one of the greatest men who ever lived. *Aderes Eliyahu*, the cloak of Elijah — that was enough; the hint, the gesture of a great man must be taken seriously, Elisha knew. Such things have meaning. I cannot ignore the call.

A *talmid* of the Chofetz Chaim relates the story of his parting from his Rebbe. As a young man, when he left the *yeshiva* in Radun, he went in to the Chofetz Chaim to say farewell and to request a *bracha* (blessing). As he entered the Chofetz Chaim's presence, before he could say anything, the Chofetz Chaim said to him:

"I am a *Kohen*."

The *talmid* was frozen — what was the Chofetz Chaim telling him?

Continued the Chofetz Chaim "And you are not. Do you know what that means? I shall tell you. When the *mashiach* arrives and the *Beis Hamikdash* (Temple) is rebuilt, we shall all be running towards it. When you reach the gates, they will say to you 'You cannot enter, you are not a *Kohen*.' But I shall be allowed to enter. Do you know why? Because thousands of years ago, in the Sinai desert, a great sin was committed and Hashem's honor had to be avenged. Moshe stood and called '*Mi la'Shem eilai* — Who is for Hashem: to me!' The people of Levi, my ancestors, responded immediately and ran to his side. Yours did not. And therefore I am descended from *Kohanim* and you are not; that is the result and that is the difference between us."

And after a pause, his final words to his speechless *talmid:*

"Sometime, somewhere, in your life out there in the world, you will hear a call '*Mi la'Shem eilai* — Who is for Hashem: to me!' When you hear that call — run!"

Chapter 13

The Importance of Beginnings
Rosh Hashana

A s the energy of time cycles through its phases, it reaches peaks which are specific to its seasons. The energy which lends itself to inspiring and re-vitalizing the "point of beginning" peaks at Rosh Hashana, the New Year. One who wishes to elevate and amplify his power of new creation, his ability to be always new and self-generating, should utilize the spiritual power of Rosh Hashana to the full. Let us delve into the idea of Rosh Hashana to discover the energies which are manifest then in order to be able to best use this opportunity. Strengthening the inspiration of the first phase of experience is the key to building the strength and stamina needed for the second, the phase of diminished inspiration.

Rosh Hashana is the beginning of the year. The spiritual forces operating at moments of beginning are unique. *"Hakol holech achar harosh* — Everything goes after the beginning"*: the entire course of any process is determined by its beginning. This is because a beginning is a conception, and conception represents the laying down of the genes which are the blueprint for *everything* which is built later. The spiritual rule is that the closer to the moment of conception, the more potent and critical the forces: a small injury to the human body may not be of major significance in an adult; a fetus during its development is much more sensitive to such an event; and a minute change to the genes may have the most far-reaching results imaginable.

At the moment of conception all details are being coded most potently; it is therefore the most critical moment. No subsequent moment can ever have the intensity and significance of that first moment. The flash of conception contains everything, all later development is simply a revelation of what was created during that first flash.

*　　*　　*

Rosh Hashana is the conception of the year and the next ten days are its gestation. That is why these days are so critical to the whole year. That is why a person is judged for *the entire year* as he appears on Rosh Hashana — the personality as it exists then is the core; it will take supreme effort later to change. Change on Rosh Hashana is much easier — one can manipulate the "genes" of one's character then. People of spiritual knowledge take extreme care to live perfectly on Rosh Hashana — the year is being conceived. Many have a custom not to sleep at least during the morning hours; they wish to lay down the genes of the year in consciousness, not oblivion.

What is the source of this special energy? The first Rosh Hashana ever, which of course must represent its true nature most powerfully, was the day of the Creation of man. That day of Creation was the world's first Rosh Hashana and its climactic event was the Creation of the human. That is why the day always retains its power to *re-create* man! When we genuinely and intensely decide to elevate our personalities on Rosh Hashana, become inspired to live the coming year as higher beings, we are using the day's deeply-rooted energy as the day of human creation. The day has the power to energize real change and help a person become unrecognizably different.

*   *   *

There is an idea that Adam was created at the very place which would later be the *mizbeach* (altar) in the Temple. *"Adam mi'makom kaparaso nivra* — Adam was created from the place of his atonement"*. His very first moment of life was generated from earth which was gathered from all parts of the world but which was concentrated on the one spot which would later become the site of sacrifices — that activity which most powerfully atones and brings man close to the Divine. His moment of creation is at once the most intense newness possible and also contains the element of the most intense change possible — from sin to atonement, which is really new creation itself. Hence the unfathomable power of Rosh Hashana to help us become new. Little wonder that the mystical custom is to minimize sleep!

*   *   *

The service of the day reflects this idea of reaching for the root. The order of prayer is based on *Malchuyos* (kingship), *Zichronos* (memory) and *Shofros* (*shofar*-blowing).

THE IMPORTANCE OF BEGINNINGS / 139

Malchuyos (kingship) represents the effort of renewing the root of all Creation and all service — establishing that Hashem's rule is absolute and primary. *Before* accepting the yoke of specific *mitzvos* we must accept Hashem's kingship in general, as expressed in the famous *mashal* (allegory) of a great king who was asked to decree laws for a country. The king agreed only on condition that the people first accept his sovereignty over them; only then would his laws be binding and meaningful. The root of Creation is Hashem's kingship, and so too is the root of all spiritual growth. This realization is the most primary of all on Rosh Hashana and it requires a delving into the deepest level of *ratzon* (desire) during the prayer service to reach the consciousness of and desire for Hashem's complete rule.

Zichronos (memory) represents the idea of remembering in true spiritual depth the points of origin of the world and of the Jewish people and its destiny. This deep form of memory is a re-entering of the male phase of new conception — to go back to the initial flash or spark and re-live it vividly and literally. The root of זכור *zachor*, "remember", is identical with זכר "male". The connection should be obvious. Maleness is exactly that: a carrying over of the distilled essence of all previous generations in a seed which will form the next generation. The seed is a "memory" of the past. In fact the word זכרן "memory" and זרע "seed" are numerically equivalent. The work of memory, re-living the flash of creation, is perfectly fitting and necessary for Rosh Hashana.

Shofros (*shofar*-blowing) indicates, along the lines we have been discussing, reaching for the heart, reaching for the root of the *neshama* and the personality. The essence of the *shofar* is that it has a voice but no words. The mystics explain that the voice is the root of speech and contains far more than the individual finite words. Words may convey information, but the voice conveys the person. This is why prophecy is referred to as "voice", not words: when Hashem tells Avraham to listen to Sarah's prophetic advice the verse says "Shma b'kola — Listen to her *voice*", not "Listen to her words".

Hashem tells the prophet "Kra b'garon, al tachsoch — Cry out in your *throat*, do not hold back"; prophecy is not from the mouth, the origin of words, but from the throat, the origin of raw sound. The blessing we pronounce on hearing the *shofar* is "lishmo'a kol shofar", to "hear the *voice* of the *shofar*". The *shofar* is raw sound, a raw cry, and that is why it has the power to open the *neshama*. All the words in the world cannot convey the emotion of a scream of a child in the night. The *shofar* is that scream.

*   *   *

Rosh Hashana correctly lived should leave one supercharged. The energy achieved should be so great that the rest of the year can be lived accordingly — not as a *continuation* but as a *constant experience of newness!* Spark must become flame and that flame must spark a new blaze; always. That is Jewish living. There is a mystical idea that being alive today because one was alive yesterday is called dying. Being really alive means that one's life is *generated* today, not as a passive result of the past but as an explosion of newness now and always.

The Hebrew root אני meaning "I" has two fascinating derivatives, אנא *ana* and אין *ayin*. The word *ayin* means "is not", *ana* is much harder to translate — it indicates an inexpressible pleading or longing as in "Ana Hashem hoshi'a na", the longing for redemption. These words, *ayin* "is not", and *ana*, intense hope for the future, also mean "from where" and "to where". When one asks "Where have you come from?" one says *me'ayin ba'ta*. When one says "Where are you going?" one says *ana telech* (or *le'an*). But incredibly, if one stops to consider the literal meaning of these expressions, a most inspiring depth becomes apparent: *me'ayin ba'ta* — "From where have you come?" literally means "You come from nothingness"! And *ana telech* — "Where are you going?" literally means "You are going to an inexpressibly great dimension"!

Hebrew, the language of holiness, is pregnant with spiritual depth. The simple, mundane idea of a person arriving from some previous place is expressed in common Hebrew as the transition from nothingness to his present state (*yesh me'ayin* — something from nothing!) In other words, the spiritual grasp of this moment is that it is relative to the previous moment as existence compared to nothingness! *That* is newness! And from this moment to the next the explosion is so great that it cannot be translated! That is the striving of a spiritually sensitive person, to generate new inner life continually.

Avraham Avinu says of himself *"Va'anochi afar va'efer* — And I am dust and ashes"*. Torah is never mere poetry, every nuance has infinite meaning. What is the meaning of "dust and ashes"?

The idea is this. Ashes are the bare elements left when a substance has been completely burned. "Dust" of the earth is the rich soil in which growth takes place. Avraham, who most profoundly represents the idea of newness, of being the father, the founder of the Jewish people, who forged a whole new way of living, sees himself as constantly incinerating what he has become in order to use those elements as soil for new growth. No element of his development is allowed to continue passively, here today because it was here yesterday. All of his being is distilled into a memory which is the nucleus for a new birth — constantly! That is the power of *chiddush*, self-generating newness, the source of spiritual life and growth.

Chapter 14

Faster than Time
Pesach

L et us look more deeply into the energy of beginnings. Both Rosh Hashana and Pesach are beginnings of the year. Rosh Hashana is the occasion of new creation of the human as an individual; Pesach is the occasion of new creation of the Jewish people. What can we learn from this observation?

The spiritual forces operating at Pesach time each year are such that the Jewish people and in fact any individual Jew can achieve the impossible if these forces are used. An attempt to leap up, to reach a whole new level of sensitivity, of personality development, can have a degree of success if undertaken on Pesach which may be far more difficult at any other time.

There is a special Divine assistance offered at this time which makes achievement of many levels of growth possible in one leap; under normal circumstances such levels must be painstakingly acquired in gradual sequence. The very word

"Pesach" means "leaping over"; at a deeper level the connotation is that of leaping over *levels of growth* which would ordinarily have to be attained one at a time.

This energy is particularly strong on the first night of Pesach; it is a time of most intense inspiration. Mystical sources indicate that on all other nights our *ma'ariv* (evening prayer) builds certain connections in the higher worlds; on the first night of Pesach these are built automatically, our work is not needed. Why do we *daven ma'ariv* (pray the evening service) on *seder* night, then? In order to *connect ourselves* with what is happening in the higher worlds! To bring down some of those very high energies to our level. This night needs none of the usual protection which night makes necessary — it is a *leil shimurim*, a "night of protection", we are Divinely guarded to an extent which never occurs on any other night of the year. It is truly "different from all other nights"! So let us ask, with deeper insight, the old question *"Why* is this night different from all other nights?"

*   *   *

Using the principles we have discussed previously, we can begin to understand that this night must have unparalleled power: on this night, the first *korban Pesach* (Pesach sacrifice) was eaten. The culmination of the ten plagues, the smiting of the Egyptian firstborn, occurred at midnight. Our homes were "passed over" by Hashem as He smote the Egyptians, Himself personally and not by means of angelic agents. The Exodus began, the redemption was manifest. The redemption occurred with lightning speed *(k'heref ayin* — like the blink of an eye): there was not time for the bread to rise and it was taken out of

Egypt as *matza*. Such events are surely the physical expression of indescribable energies loosed on the higher plane. What can we understand of the nature of these events and their root? What is the deeper meaning of this speed? Of the nature of *matza?*

Let us start by asking a question which has bothered some of the more recent commentaries. There is a well-known idea that the Jewish people in Egypt were on the forty-ninth level of impurity and had to be redeemed because had they remained in Egypt any longer they would have sunk to the fiftieth level, from which there is no return. The redemption occurred when it did because there would have been no Jewish people to redeem had Hashem delayed at all; we were saved at the last moment possible. This idea understands that at the very last moment in Egypt, the moment just before the Exodus, our existence was critically in the balance — one moment longer and it would have been too late.

The problem is, though: how could one more moment of time in Egypt have caused us to disappear spiritually, to fail and fall into Egyptian impurity — that last moment was the greatest moment we had ever experienced, it was the instant of highest revelation, supercharged with awareness of Hashem's closeness. That moment of midnight was incandescent with purity; it was the climax of a process which had begun months before with the first of the plagues at which time the slave-labor had ended; the subsequent plagues were appreciated by the Jews as ever-increasing revelations of Hashem's *hashgacha* (conduct of affairs); this night was the pinnacle of that process. How is it possible to conceive of the imminent disintegration of the Jewish people into impurity and oblivion by a prolongation of that state of being? It would seem that more of that intensity of revelation would have transformed people into angels!

The sources which deal with this idea understand that what is being referred to here is literally one more moment in that state; not more time in the previous phase of slavery and persecution in general, but very specifically more time on that last night in Egypt. What is the answer to this problem?

*　　*　　*

An approach to this question is found in the deeper sources. There is an idea that one can live in the physical dimensions of space and time and be subject to them, part of them; or one can live within them and yet transcend them. To do this one must minimize the contact between oneself and the physical elements. In the time dimension, this is known as *z'rizus,* zeal or alacrity in performing *mitzvos* and service of Hashem. The Maharal explains that if one moves fast, minimizes the time taken for action, one can overcome the stifling effects of time. Of course there is always a finite time needed for action, but the point is that spirituality is contradicted by *unnecessary* expansion of the physical dimensions of space and time. The minimum time needed is not a contradiction to spirituality at all, in fact zealous action elevates the physical dimensions to a spiritual level. Since the spiritual world is above time, explains the Maharal, we can make contact with it by coming as close as possible to it by our efforts, by shrinking the physical component of our actions to the absolute essential minimum.

Put another way, laziness, or the slowing down of action, the expanding of the physical dimensions, makes us part of those dimensions. Sluggishness is the opposite of spirituality. Laziness is incompatible with spiritual growth.

In terms we have used previously, what is meant here is that spiritual life is generated in the almost infinitely short-lived moment of the flash of conception, the male phase of reality. The work of the female phase is to maintain the spiritual energy of that first phase and to bring it into the finite world, but this can be done only if the creative conception phase is electric, alive, unburdened by physical heaviness.

Let us return to that moment of midnight in Egypt. The problem with more time in Egypt would not have been the contaminating effects of Egyptian impurity; that danger had long since ceased. No, the problem with more time in Egypt would have been *more time* itself! Let us strive to understand. The redemption had to occur *k'heref ayin*, in the blink of an eye because that alacrity is necessary for an event to remain spiritual. Had we left Egypt slowly, naturally, in a relaxed fashion, we would have been a natural people! The Jewish nation was being born then; the moment of birth *had* to be transcendent because "Everything goes after the beginning", we became and remain a spiritual people because our beginning was spiritual. Our moment of formation occupied the absolute minimum of time, and since then we have lived on the edge of the physical universe, at that edge which interfaces with the transcendent, the Divine. The terrible danger of more time in Egypt would have been the time itself; that is the impurity which is meant here, the impurity of a nation destined for spirituality becoming merely physical, merely natural.

*   *   *

And that is the secret of Pesach — riding the wave of

minimum time. Overriding time. We left Egypt too fast for the natural to take effect. Too fast to be in danger of becoming slowed by friction with the natural world. Too fast to be slowed into the material and the finite. Too fast for dough to rise, for the food which sustains our lives to expand into the swollen, bloated dimension.

A people only just within the physical, sustained by a food which is only just the sum of its ingredients.

If we think a little further: what is *matza*, one of the central *mitzvos* of Pesach? What is the difference between *chametz* (leaven) and *matza?* Only time! Not a difference in ingredients, only a difference in time. Flour and water if baked within a certain minimum time become *matza*. A second's delay beyond that minimum: *chametz*. Just as the letters of the very words *chametz* and *matza* differ by only the most minimal speck of ink (the difference between the ח of חמץ and the ה of מצה), so too they themselves differ by only a speck of time.

And what a difference: eating *matza* is a positive *mitzva* of the Torah, its reward is immeasurable. Eating *chametz* is a prohibition of the Torah and its punishment is *kares*, spiritual excision! Literally the difference between life and death, rooted in a few seconds of time.

*   *   *

This is the secret of the statement of the Sages: *"Mitzva haba'a leyad'cha, al tachmitzena* — When a *mitzva* comes to your hand, do not let it become stale"*, literally "do not let it become *chametz*, sour"*. *"U'shmartem es ha'matzos* — And guard the *matzos"* can be read as "And guard the *mitzvos"*. No mere play on words; the idea here is that just as *matza* becomes *chametz* if left too long, so too a *mitzva*, spiritual life for the one who performs it, becomes *chametz*, fermented, sour, if it is allowed to become part of the natural. A *mitzva* is a physical action containing unbounded spiritual energy, but it should be performed thus. If it is performed as no more than a physical action it may lose its connection with the spiritual world. *Mitzvos* are like *matzos*: performed at the higher level, with zeal and alacrity, they are transcendent; performed sluggishly, slowly, they sour.

Physical expansion is the root from which *tum'ah*, impurity can grow both in time and space: the Egyptian sorcerers could not duplicate the plague of *kinim*, lice. The commentaries explain the reason: *kinim*, lice, are too small for the *tum'ah*, the impurity of the Egyptians' sorcery to be able to effect. *Tum'ah* operates only when there is substantial physicality! Shrink the physical, and impurity ceases to be able to take effect!

*   *   *

So we understand something of the depth of that last midnight in Egypt. With alacrity we left Egypt, shrinking the time of our birth as a people to the minimum, maintaining the potency of that moment. As the Egyptian firstborn were smitten, we were born. The moment of the Creation of the world centuries before, that activation of the *first* of Hashem's ten creative utterances was being brought to fruition in the parallel and opposite event of Egyptian "firstness", vested in the firstborn, being destroyed as our "firstness", our birth was occurring. Avraham had provided the link: sacrifice of *his* firstborn (by Sarah) as the climax of *his* ten formative trials, the merit of which had led to the Jewish people's existence. All these moments of "firstness", of birth, were being brought together, being activated for all of history at that moment which was both in time and beyond it. "Different from all other nights" indeed!

*　　*　　*

The Sfas Emes expresses the connection between that midnight of miracles and the rest of Jewish history in the most beautiful manner. He asks why we call the procedure of seder night a *"seder"* — the word *"seder"* means an "order", a regular, predictable series of events. Strange that we celebrate the most potent series of miracles, the sharpest departures from the normal order, with the name *seder*, "order"! His answer is unforgettable. For the Jewish people, our natural order is the miraculous! We have a *seder* of miracles. We were forged in impossible circumstances, conceived in a blaze of miracles, born beyond time. We can never descend into the natural; for us to do so would be souring of the worst kind, transforming *matza* to *chametz*; lethal in the extreme.

*　　*　　*

There is an idea that the phase of conception is dimensionless; the phase of continuation or maintenance is a perfect circle. The female phase of concretizing, bringing into the physical, is represented by a circle. A circle is the *only* shape possible which has no unique point; unlike any other geometric shape any of its segments is identical to all the others. From the smallest arc the rest is predictable. It has no newness at all. The danger of this phase is that it is open to staleness, to lack of creativity, to force of habit, to depression. If the female phase is maturely handled it gives expression to newness *continually*, if not it freezes, devitalizes, desensitizes. The letter of the alphabet which expresses this is of course the *samech*, a circle. The Torah teaches the idea that newness must be entirely fresh, maximally potent in the following way: in the entire description of the Creation in *Bereishis* (Genesis) there is not a single *samech*! A lengthy text written entirely without this letter! There is another *parsha* (section) in Torah which also contains no *samech:* not surprisingly it is the *parsha* of *bechor*, the laws of the firstborn!

*　　*　　*

We must live on the plane of *chiddush*, newness. We must never expand into the natural. The *first* law in the *Shulchan Aruch*, the code of Jewish law, concerns the beginning of the day, the first obligation of the day. It is fascinating that that first *halachic* obligation is to get out of bed! Understood superficially, this is good advice. But there is much more than that here: what is intended is a basic lesson in beginnings — if one is strong as a lion to arise in the morning, if one *begins* the day with no laziness, not allowing the sluggishness of natural human inertia to contaminate the moment of waking, of first consciousness, *then* the day can be spiritual, elevated!

Everything goes after the beginning! Pure beginnings, beginnings beyond time, cannot possibly provide a foothold for the negativity of staleness and depression. That is indeed the most fitting beginning for a code of Jewish law!

There is no negativity in the moment of new creation. While the energy of creativity is flowing, depression and despair are impossible. *The spiritual root of depression is lack of growth* in the personality. When time ticks away and nothing new is being built, when all is static, the *neshama* feels the cold hand of death.

The sadness of the end of life is that activity is no longer possible, no change can be generated, all is frozen. That is the essential difference between life and its opposite, and the *neshama* has a premonition of that final state when it is inactive in this world. This is a great secret in the understanding of depression, and this is the reason that *the cure for depression is activity;* at first, any purposeful activity, but leading as soon as possible to activity of the *neshama*, the movement of growth.

* * *

The first night of Pesach. Incredible energy, incredible opportunity. A time of transcendent beginning. A time to inspire children, beginners in spirituality. A time to be inspired. A time to reach for the impossible, to reach above time.

Chapter 15

Counting Days, Creating Time
Sefiras Ha'Omer

W^e have studied some of the ideas and elements which make up the spectrum of inspiration, work despite the loss of inspiration, and the result which should be a return to inspiration. With this in mind the spiritual path which leads from Pesach to Shavuos should be discernible. Let us define this path in order to understand the energies flowing down from the spiritual worlds at this time.

*   *   *

There is a *mashal* (allegory) brought by the Sages to illustrate this path and the idea that Pesach must be grasped as a totality, but *sefiras ha'omer*, the period between Pesach and Shavuos, must be grasped oppositely, as a sequence of individual parts.

A father and son were walking in a dangerous place.

They happened upon a chest of treasure. The son wanted to count out the individual gems of the treasure immediately. The father said: "It is too dangerous; we may lose all if we delay here. Let us take the chest unopened with us; when we arrive at a safe destination we shall be able to open it and count out its contents in detail."

So too, Pesach must be grasped as a leap to a new level perhaps many stages above one's present level without traversing each level individually. Thereafter the counting begins, each stage must be accounted for. What does this mean?

* * *

Pesach, as we have seen from more than one perspective, is a time of explosive potential, of opportunity to achieve what is ordinarily impossible. After the uplift of Pesach comes the difficult time of *sefiras ha'omer*, the counting of the *omer*. This is the period of forty-nine days leading to Shavuos, the time of *matan Torah*, the giving of the Torah. The *mitzva* of this phase of the year is to count the days between Pesach and Shavuos. What is not so readily understood is: what does counting accomplish? What is built in the *neshama* and the world by counting days or stages? How does the work of counting result in the *simcha* (happiness) of Shavuos?

Let us begin by noting a fascinating difficulty which arises from an opinion of the Ramban concerning this *mitzva*. The Ramban holds that this is one of those *mitzvos* which are not *she'ha'zman grama* — not caused by time. There are *mitzvos* which are time-bound, occasioned by time; such a *mitzva* must be performed at a particular time because that time demands that particular *mitzva*, that time is in a sense the cause of the *mitzva*. Now it is hard to imagine a *mitzva* more time-bound, more time-defined than *sefiras ha'omer*! It is performed specifically between Pesach and Shavuos, daily at the beginning of each twenty-four hour period, at nightfall. It is entirely a *mitzva* of time, it marks the passage of the days from Pesach to Shavuos. How can the Ramban possibly understand that this is not a *mitzvas eseh she'ha'zman grama* — not a *mitzva* which is caused by time? The very word "Shavuos" means "weeks" — it is the result of having counted seven weeks from Pesach. Can there be *anything* about this *mitzva* which is not time-bound?

* * *

Before attempting to answer this most perplexing question, let us ask one or two others. The conventional understanding is that counting the *omer* is a "count-down", a counting of the days remaining until Shavuos — this is a natural activity of one who anticipates a longed-for event. When one looks forward to a significant day one counts off the days remaining between the present and that day. Why then do we count the days which have elapsed from Pesach? Surely we should be counting the diminishing number of days remaining until Shavuos, each day one less, rather than an increasing count of the days which have passed? The fact is that in *sefiras ha'omer* we count up — one day of the *omer*, two days of the *omer*, and so on. Why?

Another facet of this same observation is as follows: we are counting towards Shavuos and yet we call the count *sefiras ha'omer* — the counting of the *omer* which is the offering brought on Pesach! Why is the *mitzva* named for the point of departure instead of the goal? The concept of these seven weeks is certainly a development — from the coarser offering of the barley *omer* on Pesach to the refined flour offering on Shavuos; in fact, the commentaries point out that barley is animal food, fine flour is human food — the idea is that of taking the lower, undeveloped animal self and elevating it in stages. If the path is one of growth towards a higher state, why focus backwards? These are fundamental questions concerning this *mitzva*.

*   *   *

Let us understand. The *chiddush* (novel idea) to grasp here is that counting, in Torah terms, is not a sentimental marking of the passage of time until a goal; it is the *building of that goal*. Counting is work. Counting means *accounting* for and developing each component of a process fully, responsibly, and in correct sequence. Only when each detail is painstakingly created and assembled into the process can the goal be reached — in fact that itself is the goal; the sequence is our responsibility, if it is done correctly, the goal certainly results. The goal itself, in spiritual terms, cannot be built or achieved directly — it is transcendent. But the finite components can be built; when that is done appropriately, the result manifests as a gift.

An analogy would be as follows: music is a deep and wonderful example of the beauty which can be perceived in the world. A musical experience is certainly greater than the sum of its parts, the individual notes which must be played to produce that music. One is moved by the totality of the music, the interrelationship and harmony of the notes which combine to produce the unique quality of the music as a whole. But that effect is achieved *by playing those individual notes* — each note must be the correct one, played at the correct time — and the music results! One cannot produce music "as a whole" in one single action — one can only execute each individual tiny component faithfully and accurately; when this is carefully done, music is the result.

This analogy is not accidental — music is made of seven notes (the eighth in the octave is the same as the first) which combine to produce far more than could ever be imagined from hearing them individually. *Sefiras ha'omer* counts seven weeks of seven days and mystically these elements and the elements of music are based on the same source. In fact, the mystical term which describes the deepest source of the seven elements on which the physical world is based is *sefiros*, which literally means elements of counting! (*"S'for"* is to count, the root of *"mispar"*, a number.) The world itself is based on a counting, a combining of specific sub-units in specific ways to produce the whole of the Universe. One can begin to understand what is meant by "the music of the spheres"!

* * *

Music provides an even deeper insight into our subject. Mystically, one can achieve a merging into the oneness or totality of Creation by properly understanding the construction of its parts; in music there is the potential to feel this in some rarefied way. It states that when the prophet needed inspiration in order to prophesy he called for music — the conventional understanding here is that music soothes and uplifts, necessary conditions for prophecy.

But it is much deeper than that. Music is an expression of

the perfect harmony of individual components necessary to produce a new entity, a new experience. *That* is a necessary condition for prophecy, to take the finite components of physical life and use them to become a vessel for holiness, for revelation. In fact the words used there are *"Ve'haya k'nagen ha'menagen* — When the musician played"*, prophecy was achieved. But close attention to the words yields a sharper translation: *"Ve'haya k'nagen ha'menagen* — When the musician *became the music"!* Then prophecy was indeed achieved!

These ideas are exceedingly difficult to put into words, as we have noted elsewhere. The words remain individual, isolated notes. They must be played correctly to be heard.

*   *   *

Sefiras ha'omer is such a counting. The transcendence of Shavuos, Torah, is reached not by a single act which builds it, but by a deliberate painstaking building of each of the seven days of the seven weeks which leads to it. When that is done, *Shavuos results.* We work on the process, the pathway, not on the result, and the result happens of its own.

The clearest illustration of this is that the Torah commands "You shall count fifty days" and yet we count only forty-nine. Why? Why do we not actually count the fiftieth day on Shavuos itself as the words clearly indicate? The answer is striking: we cannot count the fiftieth; it is pure transcendence, of another world entirely, beyond finite counting. It is Shavuos, the giving of the Torah. We would be limiting it by assigning it a finite number. It is not an element, it is totality. We can count the forty-nine finite, human stages; when we do so, Shavuos and transcendence arrive as a gift, as the amazing result of our attention to the fragments. In fact, we *fulfil* the Torah's command to count the fiftieth day *by not counting it,* by not limiting it to a finite number! That is the *only* way to reach Shavuos — to do *all that we can* and then to *allow* the *kedusha* to manifest.

That is the nature of the spiritual — it takes effect on the correctly-used and prepared physical; it is the totality and the oneness which far transcends the sum of its miniscule parts. We count forty-nine, Hashem counts the fiftieth.

*　　*　　*

And that is why we count *from* Pesach and not *towards* Shavuos. We cannot *cause* Shavuos; we can build the path. We build on the *omer,* on what we have as a beginning at Pesach. That is our focus: "Today is one day of the *omer*" — we have *built* one day; "Today is two days of the *omer*" — we have *built* two days. When we have built forty-nine correctly, *Shavuos takes over!* And we and our counting *become* a higher reality, "*Ve'haya k'nagen ha'menagen*".

Counting is building. Some count specifically the personality traits in their seven sub-units of seven categories over the *sefira* weeks and work on each one intensely on its appropriate day — a real "riding of the wave" of time which can be done at this time of year. But even without this specific intention, the counting itself builds. There is an idea that when a woman counts the *zayin neki'im,* the seven days leading to the higher level she achieves with the *mikva* experience, she should actually count the days — not just assure that the required time interval has passed but actively and consciously *count* each day; the counting is building that level.

COUNTING DAYS, CREATING TIME / 161

*   *   *

That is why we count from Pesach rather than towards
Shavuos; that is why Shavuos is called "Weeks", *named* for the very
time we have counted; and that is a clue regarding why the
mystical *sefiros* are thus named — the "countings" of the world.

Perhaps now we can return to the problem with which we
struggled in the startling opinion of the Ramban that *sefiras
ha'omer* is not a time-caused *mitzva*. The Ramban is here
revealing a most remarkable idea: the Torah is teaching us that
contrary to what we may understand, time is not necessarily a
fixed entity which causes certain changes and events; this time
is here — it demands, causes, a certain response. Not
necessarily. Rather, our actions, our *mitzvos* may be a deeper
root yet. Not as we are used to thinking, that time is *"k'via
ve'kayma"* — fixed and established; no, it may be *dependent on
us*. Put most sharply, *sefiras ha'omer* is not a *mitzva* which is
caused by time, but rather, time is caused by *sefiras ha'omer!* Our
counting builds the reality!

What a breathtaking flash of insight into the creative,
causative power of Torah and *mitzvos* as the real *"k'via
ve'kayma"*, the underlying fixed basis of reality.

*   *   *

And what an insight into the spiritual path. We do not wait
for events to happen to us, for the uplift and blessing of the
seasons and their holiness to come to us, we must build those
things; we do not remain stationary in time as it washes over
us, we must move forward actively to greet those great
moments. The mystics say that if one waits for *kedusha*, holiness,

it may be long delayed. One must go towards it; then it rushes toward the seeker.

In the dimension of space we find this: on the *regalim,* the festivals of Pesach, Shavuos and Succos we have the *mitzva* of *aliya l'regel* — going, travelling *towards* the *Beis Hamikdash,* the center of *kedusha* in the space dimension. And specifically on those occasions, each one a focus of *kedusha* in time.

The mystics had a custom of going out into the fields to greet the Shabbos; we say *"Likras Shabbos l'chu v'neilcha* — To greet the Shabbos let us *go* (towards it)."* Shabbos, the center of *kedusha* in time, must be sought, must be approached, must be *moved towards.* That is the only way for it to be *"m'kor ha'bracha",* the source of blessing.

*   *   *

Counting days, creating time. We should not be passively riding time; we should be building our lives, causing time to become real. Passively drifting through time allows time inexorably to dissolve life; building life by building its elements consciously and actively in *kedusha* causes time to transcend into eternity, and ourselves to become one with that great music.

Chapter 16

The Real Existence
Shabbos

S habbos is central to Torah and Jewish living. It must reflect the fundamental pattern we are studying. The week begins and ends with Shabbos — an inspired beginning, a week of work and an inspired end to the week. From the holy to the ordinary to the holy again.

What is the message of this weekly cycle? What energies are being manifest in it that we should be using, riding? Why do we need a Shabbos every week whereas other *mo'adim* (festivals) occur only yearly? There must be a most essential lesson for the *neshama* (soul) in Shabbos which necessitates such close repetition.

*   *   *

There are many ideas in Shabbos, but perhaps the most basic is that it represents an end-point, the *tachlis* of a process.

The week is a period of working, building; Shabbos is the *cessation* of that building, which brings home the significance and sense of achievement that building has generated. It is not simply rest, inactivity. It is the celebration of the work which has been completed. Whenever the Torah mentions Shabbos it first mentions six days of work — the idea is that Shabbos occurs only after, *because of*, the work.

A process must have an end-point to give it meaning. If work never achieves a result, the work is foolish. If an inventor builds a machine which maintains itself fully — fuels itself, oils itself, cleans itself — that is clever; provided that the machine *produces* something useful. A machine whose only output is its own maintenance would be ridiculous.

The result justifies the work, the end-point justifies the process. The pleasure of the freedom and relaxation which accompany an end-point are the direct results of the satisfaction of knowing that the job has been done. That is the real happiness, the happiness of achievement. Shabbos is wonderful if a person has a week's work to show for that week — then the relaxation is rich and full.

The Sages make the strange statement that a *talmid chacham*, a person learned in Torah, is called "Shabbos". What is the meaning of this? The underlying idea is that Torah is the ultimate end-point; the entire world was created only so that Torah could be manifest. Torah is learned *for its own sake*, not as a means to an end; it is the end, not the means. And therefore one who learns Torah correctly, one who is imbued with Torah knowledge has an aura of Shabbos about him. He is steeped in the dimension of *tachlis*, the dimension of the goal realized. There is the deepest connection between Torah and Shabbos.

So Shabbos teaches that all work must be directed to a goal.

Travelling must be towards the traveller's destination — if not, it is merely wandering. This message alone would justify weekly repetition — we need constant awareness that each of our activities must be aimed at meaningful growth. No business enterprise is run randomly — great care is taken to keep the activities of a business concern "on track", directed towards fulfilling the aims of the company. Our lives deserve at least that degree of good management!

*　　*　　*

But there is much more. Not only do we begin the week rested and inspired by Shabbos aiming to arrive at a higher, more developed state seven days later; we must remain aware that the entire span of our lives is patterned thus: born from a higher dimension, given our time here to work, to give, to achieve, we are aiming at a return to the higher dimension with a lifetime of hard work to our credit. This life is the week, the rest is the great Shabbos. Shabbos occurs weekly to teach that very fact: ultimately, sooner or later, there will be a final end to the work-phase and the long Shabbos will begin.

The illusion of immortality which we allow ourselves is powerful — I have forever to live. We never have more than seven days before we are reminded: remember Shabbos.

*　　*　　*

Let us think into this idea. There are many parallels between Shabbos and *olam ha'ba*, the world-to-come. We prepare for Shabbos on *erev* Shabbos, Friday, in ways very similar to the way a person whose life has ended is prepared for that final voyage: washed, nails trimmed, dressed in white. We prepare everything which will be needed for Shabbos beforehand: when the sun sets one cannot prepare any longer. On Shabbos creative activity in the physical sphere is frozen; the message is that after the final transition from this world to the next, no more building or preparing can be done. In the next world a *neshama* must remain at the level which was attained during life. The ecstasy of that existence is the sense of being which has resulted from a lifetime of work. There one exists face-to-face, as it were, with one's own genuine personality; no illusions, no facade protect one from reality. What has been built in the personality is real there, in fact all the raw materials which one was given in this world are stripped away, all that remains is the *increase*, the change which has been achieved using that raw material. That is the substance of the next world.

Conversely, the pain of the next world is the sensation of lack; lack of those parts of the *neshama*, lack of those *middos* (personality traits), lack of those refinements which one could have, should have, acquired in this life. Again, it is simply the experiencing of one's own reality with no buffer, no protective layers intervening.

That is the great Shabbos. Activity frozen, a sense of the results of a lifetime made clear. What was prepared is now real. What was not prepared is forever lost. That world is an ocean voyage; provisions taken along are available, enjoyed. Provisions not taken are simply not available there.

* * *

The parallel is deeper. One of the remarkable features of Shabbos is that things are on Shabbos as they are at the moment of its beginning. For example, *muktza* (*muktza* objects are those which, being unnecessary for Shabbos, may not be moved). An object is defined as *muktza* on Shabbos if at the moment of sunset it is *muktza*, even if a change occurs later — a table with *muktza* objects on it is itself *muktza* if those objects are there at sunset. Even if the objects are somehow subsequently *removed*, the table remains *muktza* until Shabbos is over. Things do not change on Shabbos — it is the dimension of being, not becoming. And things remain as they are as Shabbos begins.

Mystical sources state that a person's spiritual status in the next world is as it was at the moment of transition from this world to the next. Not an "average" of a lifetime's ups and downs, but rather a condition determined only by the final moment. Amazingly, this means that a lifetime spent in negativity can be corrected at the last moment of life, the negativity can be neutralized then. (Of course, waiting until then is not recommended! One may not have the chance or the ability to perform that comprehensive *teshuva*, repentance, at the last moment.) Conversely, a positive life can be seriously compromised if a person breaks faith at the end.

A certain Rabbi once explained this idea as follows: life is like a pottery class. One is given some soft clay to work. At the end of the allotted hour the clay sculpture is put on to the conveyor which takes it into the kiln to be fired. Once it is fired its form is permanent, no changes can later be made. If a person is lazy and does nothing with his clay all hour, it will be difficult to fashion something beautiful in the final seconds, but whatever is achieved will be made permanent. On the other hand, a person who spends all hour making something beautiful must take care that it is not damaged at the end — one crushing action at the last instant will result in a shapeless lump of clay being fired which will not reflect all the work put in previously.

Although this is a simplification of the process, it is true. Shabbos halts all work and preparation, things remain on Shabbos as they are at the moment of its entry; the end of life halts change, halts development, and the *neshama* remains as it was at that point.

The urgent message of Shabbos, therefore is: waste no time, build constantly, direct all your activities towards correct goals, prepare for the long voyage throughout life and keep faith always, even (and particularly) at the very end. The result will be real and permanent *oneg* Shabbos, pleasure of Shabbos, and Shabbos *menucha*, Shabbos rest.

*　　*　　*

Shabbos is described as *"me'eyn olam ha'ba"* — a small degree of the experience of the next world. There is an idea that all spiritual realities have at least one tangible counterpart in the world so that we can experience them: it would be too difficult to relate to the abstract if we could never have any direct experience of it. Sleep is a sixtieth of the death experience; a dream is a sixtieth of prophecy. Shabbos is a sixtieth of the experience of the next world.

Why specifically a sixtieth? What is unique about the proportion of one in sixty? One who has a sensitive ear will hear something very beautiful here. One in sixty is that proportion which is on the borderline of perception: in the laws of *kashrus* (permitted and forbidden foods) there is a general rule that forbidden mixtures of foods are in fact forbidden only if the admixture of the prohibited component comprises more than one part in sixty. If a drop of milk accidentally spills into a meat dish that dish would not be forbidden if less than one part in sixty were milk — the milk *cannot be tasted* in such dilution. The *halachic* borderline is set at that point where taste can be discerned.

The beautiful hint here is that Shabbos is one sixtieth of the intensity of *olam ha'ba* — it is on the borderline of taste: if one lives Shabbos correctly, one tastes the next world. If not, one will not taste it at all.

*   *   *

How is this higher taste experienced? By desisting from work. Not work in the sense of exertion, that is a serious misconception of Shabbos. What is halted on Shabbos is *melacha* — creative activity. Thirty-nine specific creative actions were needed to build the *mishkan* (Sanctuary) in the desert; these mystically parallel the activities Hashem performs to create the Universe — the *mishkan* is a microcosm, a model of the Universe. Hashem rested from His Creation, we rest from parallel creative actions. The week is built by engaging in those actions constructively, Shabbos is built by *desisting* from those very actions. The *mishkan* represents the dimension of *kedusha* (holiness) in space, Shabbos is the dimension of *kedusha* in time.

*   *   *

Shabbos comes at the end of the week. But it also begins the week. It is the beginning and the end. It begins the week as the definition of the goal, the ideal. Then follows the work of the weekdays. And then a higher Shabbos is reached; what was a goal, an ideal a week ago has become real, an acquisition now. "*Sof ma'aseh b'machshava techila* — Last in action, first in thought."

The word "*Bereishis* — In the beginning" comprises the letters ירא שבת "awe of Shabbos". The genesis dimension contains the eternal dimension. The statement of genesis is a statement of the goal.

When the Torah refers to Pesach as the *beginning* of the *omer* phase of counting, building, it calls Pesach "Shabbos"! Pesach, understood as an inspired beginning, contains an aspect of Shabbos. Just as Shabbos begins the week as its transcendent origin, Pesach begins the *weeks* of counting towards Shavuos as a higher source. The Shem Mi'Shmuel says that this is why we count the *omer* from the *second* day of Pesach, not the first — the first day of Pesach is such an elevated state that it requires no counting by us, it is a time of inspiration naturally; only after it departs do we have to begin building. Shabbos is *k'via ve'kayma*, established in time as holy from the Creation, unlike the other *mo'adim*, festivals, which depend on our fixing of the new month. Pesach has something of this aspect of transcendence; the Torah calls it "Shabbos".

The Torah mentions Shabbos immediately after the building of the *mishkan* to teach how Shabbos is to be kept: these actions which you have just performed to build the holiness of the *mishkan* must be stopped for Shabbos to be experienced.

But the Torah also mentions Shabbos *before* the instructions for the building of the *mishkan* to teach that Shabbos takes priority over the *mishkan:* do not build it on Shabbos. The building is secondary, the goal is primary.

The goal is first set, and lastly achieved. Shabbos is the plan and the result. It is the life of the week, the spark of *kedusha* which animates time.

*　*　*

Shabbos rest is an opportunity for introspection. What have I achieved this week? How am I better, more aware, more sensitive? Where do I need to develop in particular? Stocktaking; facing up to oneself honestly. This itself is a faint reflection of the eternal facing up to oneself which is of the essence of the next world. The meditation of Shabbos is the meditation of being, not becoming. But from that awareness the next week's "becoming" is generated.

*　*　*

Shabbos ends with *havdala*, the ceremony of "distinguishing" the holy from the mundane. A profound lesson can be learned from *havdala* which is part of the theme we have been studying.

Shabbos exits, the week begins. There is a natural sense of let-down, holiness has left, the lower state is experienced. This is why we smell spices at *havdala* — to revive the wilting *neshama*.

But a deep secret is revealed here: we take wine for *havdala*! Wine is used when *elevation* occurs, as we have noted already. What is the meaning of this paradox?

The idea is as follows. Certainly the week begins with the sadness of sensing Shabbos fade. The relinquishing of *kedusha* is palpable. We smell spices. But the week's beginning means a new opportunity to build, to elevate our present status towards another Shabbos which will be higher than the last, which will reflect another week of work and growth *added* to all the previous ones! We take wine! This is called a *"yerida l'tzorech aliya* — a descent for the purpose of elevation", a higher and greater elevation than before.

*　　*　　*

Shabbos is closely related to the idea of *teshuva* (repentance, the *mitzva* of correcting past mistakes). The letters of שבת Shabbos are also those of תשב the root of *teshuva*. Shabbos is the celebration of the remembrance of Creation, a return to the primal, perfect state, a return to the source. *Teshuva* is a return to the pure state, the state which existed before sin caused its damage. But more than this: just as each Shabbos is built by a descent from the previous one into the work of the week, just as each Shabbos is the result of the work of that week, so too the state of *teshuva* is in one way *higher* than the original unblemished state which preceded sin.

Teshuva, when motivated and performed correctly, transforms sin into merit! The mechanism of this seeming paradox is this: before a person sinned, the potential for that sin was latent in the personality. It was an undiscovered, unexpressed weakness waiting to break through. The act of sin revealed it and made it actual in the personality. Before the sin there was a serious deficiency in the personality, that person carried a flaw; the opportunity to sin proved that — the flaw was revealed.

The definition of *teshuva* is that when it has been sincerely performed the person has reached a state in which, if presented with the opportunity and temptation to sin again, he would not do so. The flaw has been removed! Sin revealed the weakness, *teshuva* corrected it. Amazingly, the sin was an integral part of the process of reaching a new level where the personality defect which led to that sin has been eradicated; the sin itself has been used as a tool for growth — it has been transformed into a merit!

Of course, one may not sin deliberately in order to utilize this process — in fact, sinning deliberately for this purpose blocks the path to *teshuva*. The ideal pathway is to recognize a character flaw before it manifests as sin and to eliminate it immediately — in this way development of the personality can take place without the damage of sin. But the fact remains that if a flaw is unrecognized and uncorrected and leads to sin, *teshuva* can redeem and even improve.

Our pathway again — a state unblemished by sin, a descent into the state of sin, an ascent to a new level of growth, stronger and clearer. The descent has turned out to be *"l'tzorech aliya"*, essential to ascent.

* * *

So we see our overall theme reflected most seminally in the cycle of Shabbos and the week; a high beginning, a descent, a loss of that high level of *kedusha*, but only for the purpose of being able to work, to achieve. And then the result of that work: a return to the dimension of the beginning, higher, more inspired, more sensitive; closer to that final Shabbos and better prepared.

IV.

Redemption

Chapter 17

Emes and Emuna
Truth and Faith

The relationship between *emes* and *emuna*, "truth" and "faith", is one of male and female which spans the entire Creation and underlies its destiny. In understanding this relationship lies our role in that destiny.

The Zohar states *"Ihu emes v'ihi emuna* — He is truth and she is faith". Truth is somehow a male dimension and faith female. What is the secret of this idea?

Emes, truth, is that which is clear, provable, undeniable — *seen*, if you like. *Emuna*, faith, lives in the hidden domain, the domain in which doubt is possible, it can only be *heard*, never seen. The correct and essential translation of *emuna* is not "faith" in the sense of belief but *"faithfulness"*, loyalty, (as in נאמן), as we find in many verses: *"Va'yehi yadav emuna ad bo hashamesh —* And his hands were *faithful* until the sun set"; they were *loyal* to their task, they remained in position. Obviously one cannot translate this verse using the concept of belief. Absolutely blind belief with no core of certainty, of knowledge, does not make sense. The Torah concept of *emuna* is loyalty to that which is true, not that which is imagined.

The first step is a discovery of truth. The second involves loyalty to that truth even when it is no longer openly apparent; the work is the work of loyalty. Two people dedicate themselves to each other in a covenant, emotionally strong, the bond is forged. But the test of their relationship lies in the years that follow, when difficulties present themselves — will the parties to the covenant remain loyal to that covenant, to each other, when the going is tough? Declarations of dedication are easy; living up to that dedication permanently is not.

*   *   *

First, *emes*, truth is revealed, apparent. Then it is hidden. When that happens the central *avoda*, the spiritual work, becomes *emuna*, faith. "*L'hagid ba'boker chasdecha ve'emunascha ba'leylos* — To speak of Your kindness by day and Your faith at night". Kindness is felt in revelation, but faith must be maintained when nothing is revealed. "*Ba'boker chasdecha*" — the morning, or day is perceived in the singular, as one; both high in quality, related to oneness, and brief in time as the first phase of inspiration. "*Ve'emunascha ba'leylos*" — the nights are perceived in the plural, they are distant from oneness, and they are repeated, seemingly interminable.

Avraham is commanded to sacrifice his son. The problem is not knowledge — he *knows* he must do this, Hashem Himself has commanded him and there is no certainty greater than that; the problem is *living up* to that command, going through with it, being loyal to it. The Jewish people are given a destiny at Sinai — the revelation is clear. But the test is after Sinai, when revelation fades — will we be loyal then?

Sinai was *emes*, revelation. And in that revelation the first *mitzva* of the Torah was spoken to the Jewish people — the *mitzva* of *emuna:* "I am Hashem" — and your obligation is to be forever loyal to Me. As the Ramban says *"Yihye eineinu v'libeinu sham kol hayamim* — Our eyes and our hearts must be there (Sinai) always". *Emes* is the beginning, *emuna* is the work which follows.

*   *   *

A remarkable feature of the human condition is the breakdown between *emes* and *emuna:* the one does not automatically lead to the other. One can know a thing with absolute clarity and yet choose to ignore it in practice. A smoker may know exactly what he is doing to his health and yet continue to smoke. A certain medical student relates how he treated a patient who was admitted to hospital with a particular disease which obliterates the major blood vessels if the patient smokes. The man was warned that he would lose a leg if he continued smoking; he continued, and a leg had to be amputated. When the student saw him a year later he was being wheeled along the hospital corridor with *both legs absent* — and still smoking.

This needs thought: how can one know a thing with certainty and not live it? What makes it possible for logical, intelligent people to ignore truth and live falsehood? Put another, sharper way: how can we ignore the strong imperative of truth in favor of the trivial? Very often the truth being overlooked or ignored is vital, life-saving, and the option chosen pathetic in its temporary appeal — how is this possible?

Rabbi Dessler asks this question; a smoker has two desires — the desire to live, and the desire for his next cigarette. The desire to live is stronger, of that there can be no doubt; there is no stronger desire than self-preservation, the desire for life. And yet the weaker desire, the relatively puny desire for a few minutes of gratification overcomes the stronger desire. Men will commit an immorality which provides instants of gratification and destroys lifetimes of work — how is this possible?

Rabbi Dessler's answer is profound beyond words. It is expressed in terms of our discussion on *ratzon*, desire: *ratzon* is the core, the root of the human. It is the source of all outflow, all inner life, as we have noted. It is the source; it is derived from the Source of reality and parallels the ultimate Oneness. In the personality all the facets, all the parts are derived from the single source of *ratzon*, the infinite center. That is the nature of a source.

At the level of an individual human being, *ratzon* is unity, all-encompassing oneness, the *single* source of all else. And therefore *a person can have only one ratzon at a time*. Two desires never occupy the seat of control of the mind, that is impossible. The battle of *bechira*, free will, is between desires which compete for the throne, for the highest, single point which activates all else and results in action.

And whichever *ratzon* is allowed in, allowed to seat itself in the control zone, takes over. That *ratzon* is *all there is* while it is in control, and the incredible result is that it is irrelevant whether that *ratzon* is strong or weak: it can be weak, illogical, immature, infantile — but when it occupies the throne it is king; the personality is nothing other than a mechanism for carrying out that *ratzon*.

This must be understood well for it is the secret of all behavior. When a *ratzon* is allowed to dominate, to give orders and energize the personality and behavior, at that moment there is no battle, no struggle of will. The nature of *ratzon* is single and total, it controls, it is not controlled. It initiates, it does not follow.

*   *   *

So we are creatures of breakdown; the breakdown between what we know and how we act. *Emes*, truth, does not necessarily lead to *emuna*, loyalty to that truth. *That* takes work. Even a most exquisite clarity, a genuinely knowing mind, is not guaranteed to express itself appropriately in action. Never guaranteed. The *middos*, the character, must be painstakingly trained, developed, to obey the *emes*, not the body and the emotions.

Emes is male: a flash of clarity, no ordeal. And *emuna* is female: the seed is buried in the ground, unseen, and needs nurture. *Emuna* "is *seder z'raim*" — the area of agriculture, for that is where faith must be maintained. Seeds flourish only after protracted care. While growth is hidden and birth is not yet revealed, only the loyalty of *emuna* can bridge the long gap between *emes* and the final stage of *geula*, redemption. Pregnancy is a woman's task. Birth is a woman's reward. We find that the original breakdown in the world, in the Garden at the beginning of time, was caused by woman. And the *geula* must be built by her, she has that capacity. In the merit of loyalty, *emuna*, that tenacity to survive ordeal no matter how difficult and prolonged, will *geula* be brought to the world.

Throughout Jewish history Jewish women have been the key to *geula* — in Egypt the women held strong when the men were collapsing; the women took full responsibility for the preservation and continuation of the Jewish people. The critical turning point was brought about by a little Jewish girl, not yet *bas-mitzva* — when Amram separated from Yocheved his wife in order not to bring children into a world where the males born were destined for destruction, his young daughter Miriam chided him: Pharaoh wants to destroy boys, but you are withholding boys *and girls* from the world! Amram heard, and took Yocheved again. And the child born of that union was Moshe! The very birth of the redeemer caused by a girl.

In the desert, the men sinned but the women did not. At Purim the *geula* was a woman's, Esther. At Channuka, Yehudis. "In the merit of righteous women...." Woman most directly bears the difficulty of birth, and merits thereby to be the agent of birth; the vessel of *emuna,* and the teacher of *emuna.* "He is *emes,* she is *emuna.*"

*　*　*

The *gemara,* referring to a story which is quoted in detail in the Aruch, teaches the qualities of *emes* and *emuna* and their relationship unforgettably. Let us record that discussion and analyze it. Attention must be paid to every fine detail of this powerful allegory, the story of "*Bor v'chulda* — The pit and the ferret (or wildcat)".

> A young girl was walking in a deserted place on her way to visit her father when she fell into a *bor,* a pit. She could not escape and would have died there had her cries

not been heard by a young man who happened to be passing nearby.

He approached the pit and asked who she was. She told him. Are you human? — he wanted to know. Yes, she assured him, she was human and not one of the twilight-zone creatures which inhabit the desert. Will you swear it? — he demanded. She swore. Will you marry me if I save you? — he asked. She agreed.

He lifted her out of the *bor*. He wanted to marry her then and there, but she objected, saying that it would not be proper: she would go to her father's house in her hometown and prepare, and he would come for her when they were prepared. He agreed. They decided to make a binding covenant, an engagement, between them.

But where were two witnesses to their pact to be found? In that deserted place there was no-one. They agreed to take as witnesses the only things which were there: the *bor* itself, the pit, and a *chulda*, a small but ferocious creature, which happened to be close by. They declared their commitment to each other, witnessed by the *bor* and the *chulda*, and parted.

She went home and began preparing for the wedding. He went back to his town and forgot her. He married another woman, and sometime later his wife gave birth to a child. The child fell into a *bor* and died. Subsequently another child was born. This child was bitten by a *chulda* and died.

The woman said to her husband: "Had our children been lost in natural ways I would have said nothing. But in such unusual ways? Surely there is something behind this."

Then he remembered the first woman and the original

bor and *chulda*, and told his wife the story. She insisted that he divorce her and go back to look for the woman he had deserted. He did so, and remembering the name of the town she had mentioned when they parted those years previously, he set out to find her.

When he entered the town and asked for the woman he sought, he was told that she was insane — she attacked anyone who came near her. He asked to see her and found the report to be true. But unknown to all, she had been feigning madness in order to avoid having to marry anyone other than the man to whom she had promised herself. When they were alone he mentioned *"bor v'chulda"* and she recognized him. They were married, had children and enjoyed happy lives together.

What are we being taught here? "He is *emes* and she is *emuna*." She is nothing on her own — he must give her life — he saves her. But not before asking many questions — who are you, are you human? Searching in his enquiry, detailed — this is the way of truth. She accepts him *without* questions. She owes her life to him. She commits herself, and her first lesson to him is that time must pass; they must prepare before marrying.

His initial involvement with her and genuine commitment to her is strong, but short-lived. He forgets immediately. She never does. This is the way of male and female, all too often — he thrills to newness, she thrills to enriching and deepening a relationship. He marries another. She is loyal though it is completely illogical. What hope could she have that he would ever return? That is the nature of *emuna* — when all evidence is against it, when things seem hopeless, when *emes* has long since faded from view, she is loyal. And he must find her again, learn the meaning of *emuna*. Ironically, it is not only a woman who waits for him, it is also a woman who teaches him what his loyalty should be — the woman he first marries, who must lose him in doing so; but faithfulness demands even that strength, the strength of sacrifice.

He obeys, because *emes* acknowledges the truth — that is what it is. And after the long ordeal, the terrible ordeal, the pain caused to everyone involved as a result of disloyalty, he must correct things. In the end, he does; there is harmony.

One who knows the nature of man and woman at their root will understand this story. He frees her and gives her life. She must teach him faith. They must suffer to be united.

The witnesses to a covenant: *bor v'chulda*. These witnesses are not human: the idea is that nature is constant, reliable. All of the Universe, from the planets to the atoms, all of biology, is reliable. No planet and no insect ever does what it is not supposed to do. Only people are unreliable, that is the danger and the price of free will. The Torah says *"Ha'idosi bachem hayom es hashamayim v'es ha'aretz* — I call to witness against you this day heaven and earth" when the Jewish people are forging their bond with Hashem. Heaven and earth are reliable; the message is that we must be, too.

$$*\qquad*\qquad*$$

Emuna lives in the *da'as. Emuna* must be *known*, it must be lived, it must supersede life itself. Only then can it be an agent of birth; it must *know* that *geula* will come. We speak of the redemption in the present tense when we pray: *"go'el Yisrael* — Who *redeems* Israel", not "Who *shall* redeem", because *emuna* bridges the present and the future. In *emuna, geula* is certain; if it is absolutely certain it can be experienced in the *da'as* even now. When the *emes* of Hashem's promise exists, *emuna* can speak of fulfilment of that promise in the present.

Only *emuna*, faith, flourishing in the *da'as* dimension, can pull us through. *"Ve'tzaddik be'emunaso yichye* — And the righteous person shall live by his faith". Shall indeed live, and only by faith.

*   *   *

The Tzlach, in explaining why we delve into depths in Torah which we cannot fully understand, gives a *mashal* (allegory) which can serve us most fittingly in our discussion.

> A group of people is shipwrecked on a desert island. A child is born on the island. As the child grows, one of the adults takes him aside and begins to teach him the *aleph-beis* by scratching out the shapes of the letters in the sand.
>
> "This may seem useless to you now", he tells the child, "you will have little use for these letters here. But when we are rescued, when we eventually get back to our land, you will see books. Libraries of books. In those books all the wisdom of the world is contained. And you will be able to read those books, because you have learned the letters here. Now, these letters are isolated shapes whose use is doubtful to you; but in that place they will be your keys to wisdom."

On that desert island the child can learn those letters only in faith. He cannot experience, see, their significance. He *trusts*, has faith, that they will someday be vehicles of light for him. And so too we study depths which are not readily illuminated. Or more broadly, in terms of our discussion, we must work, build, serve in faith. We do not demand instant revelation, resolution of all doubts. We tend the covered seeds of our lives knowing that they will break ground and flourish; but then, not now. When we are rescued.

Chapter 18

Mashiach and Redemption

In the sweep of human history, all that we have studied together must be expressed. Just as each individual human life consists of phases, just as the seasons of a year express changing energies, and just as the inner layers of the *neshama* (soul) manifest the same relationships, so too the macrocosmic organism of the world's history must be parallel in pattern.

A Creation of idyllic perfection, perfect happiness. A Garden suffused with Divine light; no suffering, no doubt, no death. And then a terrible fall and a seemingly interminable agony of effort in darkness and pain; far more doubt than clarity, not a glimmer of the Creation light to be seen. A few hours of revelation; thousands of years of hiddenness. And the resolution of this conflict?

Let us study the subject of *mashiach*, "the anointed", the messianic redeemer and the final redemption, keeping in mind all that we have learned.

                        *   *   *

A central feature of the messianic revelation is that it is
hidden until it happens. It cannot be predicted; no amount of
mystical delving can reveal its timing. It *must* be a surprise —
the *gemara* says, amazingly: *"Shlosha ba'in b'hesach hada'as; elu
hen: mashiach, metzia v'akrav* — Three things come when they are
not expected: *mashiach*, a "find" (the experience of finding
something unexpectedly), and a scorpion (a scorpion's sting)".

The *gemara* is here revealing to us that the element of
unexpectedness is intrinsic to the messianic idea, it must be
thus. We can begin to feel a little more deeply the meaning of
the brothers' experience as they faced Yosef and heard "I am
Yosef" — their redemption at the moment which seemed
impossible, from the last place imaginable; we are being taught
that even *knowing this* our redemption will seem logically
impossible.

                        *   *   *

This element of unpredictability pervades our thinking about
mashiach. We often refer to the *mashiach* as a "plant" and the
messianic advent as a "flowering". We say *"Es tzemach David
avdecha"* — the "plant" or "flower" of David; and *"matzmiach
yeshua"* — Who causes redemption to "flower" or flourish like
a plant. The idea here is that plants grow by seed: a seed
detaches from the parent plant and drops to earth. Superficially
this appears to be a loss of connection with the life-source. The
seed becomes buried in the earth and begins to disintegrate —
certainly not a promising development. And at the point of
greatest disintegration, a new shoot appears and a new plant

begins to grow. New life is not predictable from disintegration, the process is a paradox.

In illustrating the nature of the resurrection which will take place with the final revelation the *gemara* cites the example of a caterpillar which spins a cocoon and crawls into it to liquefy. When the lowly, blind, earthbound caterpillar has totally melted into a shapeless, gelatinous larva, suddenly the cocoon splits and a butterfly emerges — bright, ethereal, flying. It is hard to remain insensitive to such clues of paradoxical change inherent in nature.

The world's history and Jewish history manifest this pattern. Adam's experience in the Garden began with direct revelation of Hashem's presence; their relationship was immediate and direct. All too soon disintegration set in, the relationship became deeply hidden. The early generations of the world's inhabitants knew Hashem far more clearly than later generations. Jewish history began with the open miracles of the Exodus, the Sinai experience and the years of miraculous closeness to Hashem in the desert. The early generations experienced prophecy constantly. The *Shechina* (Divine presence) manifested in the *mishkan* (Sanctuary) and the first Temple. Miracles were commonplace. Then the gap widened — prophecy ended. The second Temple lacked the manifest presence of the *Shechina*. Miracles ground to a halt.

The second phase was (and is) as dark as the first was light: parallel to the dedication of the *mishkan* in the desert in a blaze of Divine revelation was the re-dedication of the second Temple at Chanukka — only after a hard-fought and bloody war was the dedication of the Temple achieved and a last miracle of one small flame manifest. The acceptance of the Torah at Sinai in open revelation was echoed later at Purim — acceptance of the

Torah in complete darkness: no miracles openly manifest, Hashem's name not even mentioned in the *megilla*.

This is always the pathway. The first *luchos ha'bris* (tablets of the Covenant) entirely Divine, miraculous; the second hewn by man and a faint echo of the first. The first Temple aglow with revelation, the second so much less that those who had seen the first wept when they saw the second.

*   *   *

The hiddenness of our final destiny has its origin early in our history. As Yaakov Avinu was dying, he gathered his sons around him, and was about to reveal to them the secret of the redemption — *"Bikesh legalos lahem es ha'ketz"*, he attempted to reveal the messianic end. As he was about to do so with the power of prophecy, the knowledge of the revelation was wrenched from his mind. He found himself unable to reveal the secret. He thought that the reason might be unworthy recipients — perhaps one of the *sh'vatim*, one of those great forebears of the tribes of Israel, his sons, was imperfect and therefore such a cosmic revelation was impossible. But a piercing assessment of each one showed him that they were in fact worthy.

He next assumed that although they were individually worthy, perhaps their *achdus*, their unity as a group, was faulty. Revelation at the highest level requires a Jewish people who are entirely united (as one person — this is how the nation was at Sinai). Perceiving his doubt concerning their unity, the brothers said *"Shma Yisrael, Hashem Elokeinu, Hashem echad"* — Hear O Israel (Yaakov), just as Hashem is one in your heart, so too is He one in our hearts with no division at all among us. Yaakov was reassured and uttered *"Baruch shem k'vod malchuso l'olam va'ed* — May the name of the glory of His kingship be blessed for ever". This declaration of Hashem's unity has been the central expression of the Jewish people ever since.

At that moment it became apparent that this is one revelation which must remain covered until its time. The reason is not because of unworthy recipients. Yaakov and his sons and their unity were perfect; Hashem's desire however, was that they were not to know in advance when the end of history would occur. This secret is deeper than prophecy. Predictions of the redemption are therefore forbidden.

It is a common and superficial error to understand that what was almost revealed at that highly-charged moment was a date. The issue was not simply a particular date in time. What Yaakov was about to reveal was a pathway; he was about to indicate to his sons and the Jewish people *how history works*. An outcome of such understanding would be the eventual date of the coming of *mashiach*, but that is not the point. The agony of not knowing is not simply because we do not have the specific date, rather it is because we cannot understand how everything in our history is inexorably forming the tapestry which the final stage will reveal as complete.

A revelation of the pathway, an understanding of *hashgacha* (Divine conduct of worldly affairs) at every turn of history would be far more illuminating than an isolated date. But that was not to be; our ordeal throughout history exists exactly because we cannot identify the mechanisms of *hashgacha*, all we can do is maintain the faith that somehow every event in our life as a people is an essential element in the building of our final happiness. We know that the seed falling to earth will sprout, but it is hard to believe until it happens.

So the seed of *mashiach* is driven underground. With this background it is possible to approach the perplexing subject of the pathway of the messianic genealogy through history. If one traces the personalities and events in Torah history which are the nodes of the messianic "plant" as they appear "above ground", as it were, one finds a remarkable thing: these glimpses of the messianic line are all problematic. They appear to be shrouded in very questionable morality indeed. Only the deepest investigation shows that hidden within seemingly immoral circumstances the pure seed is being carried. A remarkable observation: the seed of absolute purity which will ultimately bring the world to moral perfection hides within sordid soil indeed!

Let us illustrate this with a brief overview of some of the events involved. The *midrash* states *"Matzasi es David avdi —* I found David my servant", referring to the beginning of the messianic pathway. *"Heichan me'tzasiv —* where have I found him?" *"Bi'sdom —* in Sodom". The beginning of the long and tortuous path that *mashiach* must take through millennia of history is in Sodom — the heart of immorality. Sodom — so immoral that it must be destroyed entirely. The contrast is so startling it cannot be missed.

Where in Sodom is this messianic seed? In the loins of Lot. Lot will father a child, Moav, who will be the forebear of Ruth, great-grandmother of David. Lot, who fell, failed to maintain the greatness he had learned from his uncle, Avraham. Lot who chose Sodom. Lot whom the Sages identify by his name ליט—ליט is "a curse" in Aramaic.

Lot sits in Sodom, bearing within him the seed of redemption. He hosts two angels to a meal on that fateful eve of destruction: the cataclysmic destruction of Sodom is about to occur. Lot provides a meal: we have a deep tradition that the time of year was Pesach, Lot served *matza*. But the *Chumash* uses the word *mishteh*, a feast, for that meal, and the Sages with their superconscious ears hear in that word the *mishteh* which is used elsewhere — in the *megilla* of Purim, the Purim *se'uda* (meal). This requires understanding. Pesach is the festival of redemption, redemption in the light, redemption revealed, accompanied by miracles, in Nissan, the first month, the month of *nissim* (miracles), in the glow of spring. Purim is the festival of redemption too, but redemption in darkness, without revealed miracles, in the last month of the year, in the depth of winter. Together they form the full spectrum of the elements of redemption. And Lot is sitting in Sodom, on the eve of its annihilation and his *miraculous* redemption bearing *hidden* within his body the seed from which *mashiach* will sprout, and conducting a Pesach *seder* and a Purim *se'uda* in one!

In the eye of the storm, the seed of *mashiach* is poised to undergo a strange, ironic redemption. What a profound and most unpredictable laying down of the preparation for an Exodus ablaze with miracles and a Purim redemption complete with its mask!

The moral pathway becomes more complex. Lot and his daughters survive. They are alone in a cave. The daughters decide that they must have a relationship with their father, convinced that they are the last humans alive. And they do. And Moav is born. Forerunner of *mashiach*, a child of incest! Deep within this problematic event the core is pure: the *gemara* says "Gedola aveira li'shma mi'mitzva she'lo li'shma — Greater is a sin for the right reason than a *mitzva* for the wrong reason". But what a sordid and seamy cloak for a pure core!

And so it continues. Yehuda, son of Yaakov, destined to be the father of the messianic line, marries Tamar. Their progeny eventually gives rise to Boaz, who marries Ruth, descended from Lot. So we have the ancestry of Ruth from Lot and his daughter, and Boaz from Yehuda and Tamar. Is the union of Yehuda and Tamar clear and perfect, uncomplicated by moral dilemma? Not at all. Tamar's relationship with Yehuda is completely hidden — she disguises herself as a harlot in order to have a relationship with him. She does so because, informed with prophetic insight that the messianic line is to proceed through her, she waits for Shelah, Yehuda's son who has been promised to her in marriage. But when she sees that she is not being given to Shelah, she takes matters into her own hands and disguised as a harlot, waits for Yehuda at a crossroads. He sees her and "smells *gan Eden*", senses an uncontrollable force compelling him to have a relationship with this woman.

She is seen to be pregnant and assumed to have behaved immorally instead of waiting for her obligatory *mitzva* of Levirate marriage to one of the house of Yehuda. He sentences her to death, oblivious of the fact that she has performed her *mitzva* with him! She reveals the truth to him in absolute modesty, in secrecy. He acknowledges that she is greater than he. And she gives birth to Yehuda's son, who becomes the direct ancestor of Boaz.

Again, it would be hard to imagine a darker, more problematic lineage. And yet in the core — purity. A *mitzva* of *yibum* (Levirate marriage), no immorality at all, and *mashiach* moves another step through history.

*   *   *

David, the quintessential and definitive ancestor of *mashiach*. What of his birth? Remarkably, it is no less problematic; the moral purity no less hidden. Yishai (Jesse), one of the most perfect men who ever lived (the *gemara* lists him as one of those few who *never* sinned) marries and has sons. Before David is conceived, the specter of Yishai's descent is raised: he is accused of being of forbidden lineage. The reason is that his grandmother, Ruth, was a Moabite convert; the Torah prohibits taking converts from Moav. The Torah prohibition, however, applies to Moabite men only, not women; but that distinction was in question during Ruth's lifetime and was questioned again during Yishai's.

Worried that the prohibition may apply, Yishai separates from his wife, not wanting to father more children whose lineage may be blemished. His wife, with the depth of insight that only women have (just as Tamar had) knows that he is mistaken and that bringing another child to the world is a holy task for them. She disguises herself as a Canaanite maidservant (whom Yishai had married in a *halachically* permissible manner in the interim) and has a relationship with him — her own husband, unknown to him. A pure marriage relationship, but the husband unconscious of it! And David is conceived! Again, her disguise set aside, Yishai's wife is seen to be pregnant. David is born and shunned, rejected as impure, the issue of immorality. Again, the pure seed of *mashiach* seen in the worst possible light, scorned and spurned, even by his own father and brothers.

Then Shmuel (Samuel) the prophet is sent by Hashem to anoint the king of Israel. He is instructed to find the man to be

anointed among the sons of Yishai in Bet Lechem. He enters
Yishai's house and calls for his sons; it is no surprise that he has
been sent here — Yishai is a spiritual giant. And those sons are
striking too — when Shmuel sets his eyes on the oldest he is
convinced that this is the next king of Israel, father of *mashiach*
to be; but a prophetic voice deep within him speaks: he is not
the one. And he looks upon the second of Yishai's sons, again
hopeful. But again, the voice informs him that Hashem does not
see as humans do. And so on, until he has rejected all the young
men before him. Perplexed, he asks if there are any other sons.
No-one has thought of inviting David, he is tending his father's
sheep in the hills, rejected as illegitimate, secretly becoming
great in meditation and communion with Hashem, but in
human eyes the lowliest of creatures.

At Shmuel's insistence, David is brought. Shmuel looks at him
and is electrified: he is the one! David is anointed king. *"Even
ma'asu ha'bonim haysa le'rosh pinna* — The stone which the builders
rejected has become the cornerstone" — David's own words.

* * *

That is the hiddenness of the path of *mashiach*. Seemingly
relegated to the gutter of history, yet pure within. There are
many depths and layers to this strange sequence of events, but
our concept of a "hidden flower", a seed buried and
disintegrating in order to sprout is the general key. And it is the
key to understanding the final appearance of that seed in a
generation which may seem most unworthy of all. It is that
generation which will be the key to the opening of *da'as*, higher
consciousness, which the *mashiach* will bring. *"U'mal'a ha'aretz*

de'a k'mayim le'yam mechasim — And the world will be filled with *da'as*, knowledge of Hashem, like water fills the ocean."

Mashiach is the link to that higher state. "*Mashiach*" means "anointed", anointed with oil. Oil is always a symbol of a higher level: שמן oil, is a root whose letters also form שמנה, the number eight, the number of transcendence and miracle (the Channuka miracle — a miracle of oil — lasts eight days; *bris mila*, circumcision, takes place on the eighth day — the body is being enabled to transcend; the entire natural world has seven components — the eighth is always above). The same letters form נשמה *neshama*, the soul — the transcendent element in the human. And oil is poured on the head in the act of anointing; the highest part of the body, seat of the crown of royalty which is the highest symbol of elevation.

*　　*　　*

The path within history of perfection followed by breakdown has its origin at the Creation. The *Chumash*, analyzed by the Oral Tradition, presents a number of strange events in this context.

We are told that the earth was commanded to bring forth trees which taste the same as their fruit; the wood of the tree itself was to be fruit. The earth disobeyed and was later cursed for its disobedience. The sun and moon were of identical size; the moon rebelled and was shrunk to her present size. The world in general was created with the attribute of *din*, strict, exacting justice; but when Hashem "saw that it could not survive thus, he mixed mercy with the justice" and that is how the world continues. (Humans could not survive in a world where absolute justice is demanded always, we are creatures of imperfection and we must have the leniency which the admixture of mercy provides.)

The obvious questions are: how could inanimate objects disobey instructions? They have no free will. And if they *had* to change, why were they created differently first? Why did Hashem first create *din* alone and then "see" that mercy was needed? Surely He knew that beforehand?

The answer reveals something very deep. A tree which is itself fruit is the ideal condition — the deeper level here is that the world of perfection is not built on the idea of process which leads to *tachlis,* a result; *all* is *tachlis.* In that dimension the process itself is an end, not a means. We have studied this idea already. Sun and moon being equal is the ideal — the receiver being able to receive and reflect *all* of the giver's energy; in the world of perfection it is thus. A world built on exact *din* is the ideal condition — in the world of perfection it must be thus. In fact, in the world-to-come the trees will be as edible as the fruit, the moon will regain her former glory, and *din* will be manifest.

The secret we are being taught is that the initial condition is the condition of perfection; the world begins in perfection, at the highest level. *Then* there is a descent, a shrinking down to lesser proportions. Of course Hashem knew beforehand what was to be, but the point is that first the ideal is built (and taught) and then the lower or lesser reality takes over. But the imprint of perfection is never lost, the message remains, the ideal has been set. And that is why it can be regained. And that is why it *must* be regained in the end.

*   *   *

Let us return to Yaakov and his sons and analyze more

closely what was said there. When Yaakov had his prophetic insight into the path of *mashiach* blocked, the brothers said *"Shma Yisrael, Hashem Elokeinu, Hashem echad* — Hear O Israel, Hashem our G-d, Hashem is One". There is a particular depth in the word *"shma* — hear". Hearing is the sense one must use when vision is blocked. In the darkness, when one cannot see, one must listen. Ever since then, we have been in darkness regarding *mashiach's* coming, and ever since then we have been declaring *"Shma* — Hear".

Let us go deeper. The word *shma* has another literal meaning: "gather together into one", as it states *"Va'yeshama Shaul es ha'am* — And Saul gathered the nation". That is remarkable — our statement of faith in Hashem's Oneness requires a "hearing" which is itself an act of generating unity.

In order to understand this key concept, let us analyze hearing and seeing in the physical in order to perceive their higher meaning. Seeing happens in the light, what is seen is clear. In Hebrew "seeing", ראיה is also "proof", ראיה — because what is seen is undeniable. Deeper than this, the elements of a scene are all perceived at once, seeing is an instant mode, all is present *together*. The scene is external, it is seen "outside" of oneself.

But hearing is opposite — it happens in the dark. Most importantly, what is heard is not heard at once: the elements of sound are heard *in sequence*, over time, and they must be assembled by the listener. Hearing is internal, what is heard depends on how the listener puts together, interprets, the elements of sound. One cannot hear all the syllables of a sentence, or even one word, together — the result would be noise. One must hear one syllable, by itself meaningless, then the next. By the time one hears the second syllable, the first has faded into memory. And when the third is heard, the second has faded. And so on. When the entire sentence is completed, the elements are combined *within the listener* and understood. A dark and subjective process indeed.

What is seen is proved. What is heard can be denied. In a world of seeing, only *emes*, truth, exists. In a world of hearing, *emuna*, faith, has a place.

The mystics explain that seeing is much higher than hearing; the next world is a world which is seen, in this world one must hear. The depth of this idea is that this is a world of *process*, of *movement towards*. In fact the name ארץ *aretz*, the land or the world, is based on רץ to run or move, whereas the name שמים, *shamayim*, Heaven, is based on the word שם, meaning "there". The higher dimension is all "there", no "going towards" is possible there (relatively speaking) because that is the *tachlis*, that is *having arrived!* This world is all movement towards, the next is all goal; this world moves through time since it is all process, the next world is beyond time because all is one there.

*   *   *

This idea is the key which opens some extremely difficult areas. If one understands that what is *heard* in this world is *seen* in the world of revelation, perplexing *p'sukim* (verses) begin to be accessible. *"V'ra'u kol basar yachdav ki pi Hashem diber* — And all flesh shall *see* together that Hashem's mouth has spoken". Surely it should state that all flesh shall *hear!* One does not see speech! But in that world of revelation, one certainly does. What is heard now will be seen then. (And even the "flesh", the lowest component of the human dimension, will be able to see. And of course *yachdav,* "together" — unity is a prerequisite.)

An even more striking example than this perplexes many: at the giving of the Torah the *Chumash* states explicitly *"ro'im es ha' kolos"* — the Divine *shofar* sounds at Sinai were seen! Sounds that are visible! But we can approach this remarkable description with our principle. The idea is that at Sinai, Hashem Himself appeared. The higher world, the next world, was manifest right here in this world — this world melted into the higher existence. That is why it states that all the people present *died* when Hashem spoke (and had to be revived) — they entered the higher world as it became manifest. And that is why it states that when Hashem appeared nothing in the world moved — of course not: when the higher world manifests, when the domain of *tachlis,* of end-point is revealed, *nothing can possibly move,* there is nowhere to go! Everything is already *there!*

Now sound is possible in this world, the world of time and process. But in the higher world *sound is not possible,* there is no time, no sequence of events one following the next; all *is* at once. The only modality possible there is seeing. And therefore, when Hashem brought His Presence into contact with the finite world, as it were, when this world was elevated to the level of the next at that indescribable moment at Sinai, *only seeing was possible* — the *shofar* sounds were seen! What an exhilaration of understanding the deeper wisdom provides!

* * *

And so *"Shma Yisrael"* is our creed; hearing correctly is our work. Seeing will be the reward. Free choice exists now — one is free to hear or not to hear. Free choice has no place in the higher world — when one sees one cannot deny.

There is a very deep and wonderful idea that language was clear originally — the world was created by Hashem's *speaking* it into existence. And humans perceived the words; in fact the world and existence within it form a dialogue. With unclouded, prophetic perception all objects in the world are seen to *speak* their message clearly. (An "object" in Hebrew is a *"davar"*, and so is a "word"! Every object is a *"d'var Hashem"* — a word of Hashem!)

The world was alive with this *"lashon kodesh* — holy tongue". After language broke down at the Tower of Babel, only Avraham was left with prophetic hearing — language had become a medium of obstruction, not communication. When the world united for the evil purpose of building that tower and Hashem foiled their attempt by confounding their language, the meaning is much deeper than simply the technical problem of people speaking different languages. What is meant is that language itself broke down, the higher language of prophecy collapsed, and even when people speak the same language perfect understanding is impossible.

The word *"bavel"* (Babel) *means* a "babble" of language — the verse states *"Hava nerda v'navla sham s'fasam* — Let Us go down and confuse (*bavel*) their language". The unity of man, that absolute requirement for relating to the Unity of Hashem, was destroyed by destroying language! The very medium of revelation was transformed into a means of hiding. And the geographical location of this breakdown of language? Babylon — *Bavel!* Much later, we were exiled and prophecy was lost altogether. Where was this second breakdown of language into complete darkness? *Bavel* — the Babylonian exile! The Sages say that just as a woman is sent back to her father's house when a marriage fails, so too we were exiled to *Bavel* from *whence we came* — when language collapsed originally in that country Avraham retained prophecy and went up *from there* to Israel (Canaan). And subsequent to that second breakdown no prophecy has been heard.

Since prophecy ended, we must learn to hear even more deeply. Prophecy was revelation; in its place we have only the understanding of Torah. This is the secret of Talmud, the study of the Oral Law. Prophecy was clear, undeniable, experienced. In prophecy there is no *"hava amina"* and *"maskana"*, no "first thought" which is discarded in favor of a more accurate "second thought" or conclusion. But that is exactly the way *gemara* works; wrong ideas are examined, ground down, refined, corrected or rejected. The only tools we have are the broken pieces of truth, the shards of revelation. And so *we use those broken pieces* to reconstruct reality.

Very significantly, we study Talmud *Bavli* most intensely. We use the very breakdown, the *"bavel"* element, to bring about its repair. We cannot see any longer, we must hear. Amazingly, the Zohar, the mystical source-work (and the Talmud Yerushalmi) when introducing an argument states *"ta chazi* — Come and see". But the Talmud Bavli always states *"ta shma* — Come and hear"!

*   *   *

We can apply this idea to illuminate another difficulty. At the same time that prophecy ended, the Men of the Great Assembly composed the *brachos,* the blessings which we utter still. They composed a blessing for almost every event imaginable, every food we taste. Why were formal *brachos*, blessings, not needed before that time? How did centuries of Jews live prior to that period without a *siddur* (prayer book)?

But understanding blessings correctly in the light of our principle helps: one of the functions of a *bracha* is to identify in our consciousness the source of that bounty, that privilege, that food of which we are about to partake. Before we eat we say, as it were, "Hashem, You are the source of this apple" (*"Baruch ata* — Blessed are You" really means "You are the source of this blessing", as the Nefesh Hachaim explains).

When prophecy existed, the world was alive with the glow of prophecy. It is an error to think that the world was as it is now except that a few gifted individuals could predict the future; individuals who had prophecy could exist only in a world which had that energy flowing into it; in those generations the world was incandescent with revelation relative to the present. Every object in such a world *spoke its message*, it was a *d'var Hashem;* the dialogue between the world and the Jewish people was alive. Today an apple looks like an apple; then it glowed as a word of Hashem! One did *not need* to identify the source in the way which one must now, it was much more readily apparent. Today the darkness is so thick, the materialism so oppressive that one must identify Hashem as the source of each object and so we must make *brachos* on everything!

*   *   *

So we understand that the history of the world involves a great light which is dimmed; a "Creation light" which is hidden. Deep "underground" in the world and its history the pulse of final revelation is throbbing. We cannot identify it openly; where it seems to appear the mystery only deepens. But that is not our responsibility. Our responsibility is to work and to build. To live in *emuna*, in absolute loyalty. We must live in the darkness and rise above it. We must use the "broken pieces" available to us and painstakingly reconstruct them — in our personalities, our relationships, our prayers, our blessings, our lives.

We must bring the light of original Creation, original inspiration, into the darkness so powerfully that it ceases to be dark. That is life; that is living inspired.

GLOSSARY

aggada: Torah sources of more metaphysical, less halachic nature

alef-beis: alphabet

Arizal: Rabbi Yitzchak Luria (1534 - 1572) foremost kabbalist of the modern era

Aruch: Talmudic commentary in alphabetical format by Rabbi Nassan ben Yechiel (written in 1102)

Avraham Avinu: our father Abraham

bar-mitzva: age of majority for boys, 13 years

bas-mitzva: age of majority for girls, 12 years

Beis Halevi: Rabbi Yosef Dov (Yosha Ber) Soloveitchik of Brisk (1820-1892).

Beis Hamikdash: the Temple

Chazon Ish: Rabbi Avraham Yeshia Karelitz, of Lithuania and later Bnei Brak (d.1953)

chelek: portion

Chofetz Chaim: Rabbi Yisrael Meir Hacohen Kagan of Radin (d.1933)
Chumash: the Five Books of Moses

da'as: knowledge

emes: truth
emuna: faith

Gaon of Vilna: Rabbi Eliyahu ben Shlomo Zalman of Vilna (1720 - 1797)
gemara: Talmud
geula: redemption

halacha: Torah law
Hashem: lit. "the Name"; G-d

Iyar: eighth month of the year

kedusha: holiness

Maharal: Rabbi Yehuda Loewe ben Bezalel of Prague (c.1512 - 1609)
mashiach: messiah
matza: unleavened bread
megilla: scroll; the Book of Esther
Mesillas Yesharim: classic *mussar* (character-building) work by Rabbi
    Moshe Chaim Luzzatto (1707 - 1746)

midrash: Torah sources which delve deeper than the plain
 meaning of the Scriptural text
mikva: body of water for immersion according to the menstrual
    separation laws

Nefesh Hachaim: Rabbi Chaim of Volozhin (1749 - 1821), student of the
    Vilna Gaon
neshama: soul
Nissan: seventh month of the year

omer: barley offering brought at beginning of the seven-week period
    between Pesach and Shavuos

pasuk, p'sukim: Scriptural verses
Pesach: Passover

Rabbi Dessler: Rabbi Eliyahu Eliezer Dessler (1891 - 1954) of Russia, London and Ponovez Yeshiva in Bnei Brak
Rabbi Chaim Vital: foremost student of the Arizal
Rambam: Rabbi Moshe ben Maimon (1135 - 1204); Maimonides
Ramban: Rabbi Moshe ben Nachman (1194 - 1270); Nachmanides
Rosh Hashana: New Year

seder: Passover night ceremony
sefiras ha'omer: counting of the seven-week period between Pesach and Shavuos
Sfas Emes: Rabbi Yehuda Aryeh Leib Alter of Ger (1847 - 1903)
Shabbos: Sabbath
Shavuos: the festival of Weeks
shefa: bounty; flow of beneficence
Shem Mi'Shmuel: Rabbi Shmuel Bornstein of Sochachev (1856 - 1926)
shofar: ram's horn sounded on Rosh Hashana
simcha: joy
Sivan: ninth month of the year
Succos: festival of Booths; Tabernacles

tachlis: purpose
Tzlach: also known by the name of another of his works, the Noda Beyehuda; Rabbi Yechezkel Landau of Prague
tznius: modesty

Yaakov Avinu: our father Jacob
Yitzchak Avinu: our father Isaac